It Happened In Kansas

It Happened In Series

It Happened In Kansas

Remarkable Events That Shaped History

Sarah Smarsh

Guilford, Connecticut

Copyright © 2010 by Morris Book Publishing, LLC

Project editor: Gregory Hyman
Layout: Sue Murray
Map: Daniel Lloyd © Morris Book Publishing, LLC

Library of Congress Cataloging-in-Publication data is available on file.

ISBN 978-0-7627-5862-3

Printed in the United States of America

10 9 8 7 6 5 4 3 2 1

CONTENTS

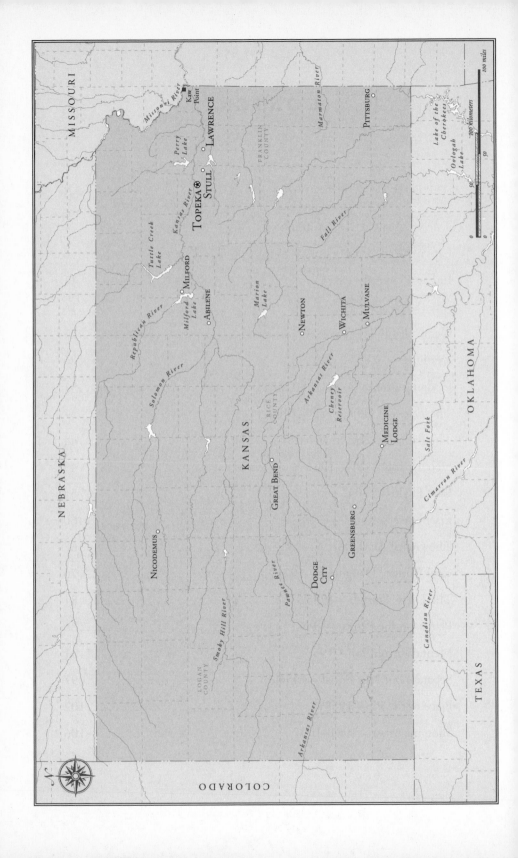

CONTENTS

Thank you to the Center for Kansas Studies at Washburn University for its research support.

INTRODUCTION

Throughout its modern history, since native tribes were driven from its eighty-two thousand square miles of grassy, windswept plains, Kansas has been a battleground of sorts. It's a state of contention rooted, perhaps, in Kansas's location at the geographical center of the United States. Wedged between the abolitionist North and the pro-slavery South, Kansas saw many bloody battles during its formative years as a free state.

True to their progressive origins, Kansans in later decades would provide a new home for former slaves fleeing the South; lend considerable momentum to the women's suffrage movement; organize historic labor strikes; invent the modern mental health hospital; lead the aircraft industry; help spearhead the lawsuit that led to desegregation; and turn a tornado-ravaged town into a world-class prototype of eco-friendly building.

Yet, with a deeply conservative and moralistic streak, Kansans also would be the first in the union to prohibit alcohol; dramatically obstruct a Wichita abortion clinic entrance for an entire summer; and vote to redefine science standards for its public schools, allowing for the teaching of creationist theories alongside evolution.

Kansas's best-known residents reveal the state's sociopolitical paradoxes: from Carrie Nation's violent crusade for Prohibition to Amelia Earhart's feminist declarations and demonstrations of her gender's capabilities; from charlatan John Brinkley's preying on rural communities to future president Dwight D. Eisenhower's steady integrity and work ethic.

Even the weather in Kansas swings from one extreme to another, offering both dry, blistering summers and unforgiving, deadly winters. Just as armed forces once fought over Kansas soil, and ideological factions have fought over Kansas's soul, weather fronts fight over its skies. Over Kansas, warm, moist air from the Gulf of Mexico clashes with cold, dry air from the north, creating the tornadoes for which the state is well known.

It's that big, swirling sky from which Kansas gets its motto, one that seems to capture the state's history of hard-won battles and progress: "Ad Astra Per Aspera," or "To the Stars Through Difficulty."

TWELVE MILE CREEK

8400 B.C.

The small, muscular men ran alongside the herd of bison, whooping and waving their spears. They had peeled about twenty of the animals from a much larger herd and now, partially clothed with pelts to block the cold, early-spring air, they swept the animals toward a nearby ravine. The bisons' hooves pounded the earth, kicking up pieces of mud as the herd veered warily from the hunters. Closer, closer. . . . Finally, one bison went over the edge, then the next. The men continued to close in, and soon the whole bunch of bison lay dead or writhing at the bottom of the ravine next to a half-frozen stretch of moving water.

The hunters hurried down the steep incline to inspect their kill, bison piled atop one another in a mangled mess of fur, horns, and hooves. The largest of the animals, a strong, impressive beast, kicked its legs at the edge of the pile. One of the men hoisted his spear, lunged, and drove into the bison the dart point he had painstakingly carved from rock. The point cut through the bison's tough flesh and found its resting place beneath a shoulder blade. The animal was still.

The men whooped to the sky, relieved that their families would have a bounty of meat and clothing. Together, they set about skinning the animals, tearing off their large legs, filleting the muscles from their backs, taking a break to sip from the creek in the grassy expanse that would become western Kansas more than ten thousand years later.

That's how it might have happened, anyway. What we know for sure is this: Someone in prehistoric western Kansas killed at least thirteen bison (more may have eroded before the discovery). And one of those bison had a projectile point behind its scapula—the discovery of which, in 1895, raised all sorts of questions about the timing of man's arrival in North America.

Many archaeologists believe that humans first arrived in Kansas and its continent around 10,000 B.C. by crossing the Bering Strait, a stretch of land that connected Siberia and Alaska toward the end of the Ice Age—invisible now, as ice melt increased sea levels and receded coastlines. Others believe people showed up much earlier, perhaps landing on the Pacific Coast in boats. However they got here, they descended from Asian ancestors and were as tough as nails. Though Kansas was no longer completely covered in ice, it was much colder than it is now, with less marked seasons. The true pioneers of this land, known as paleoindians, survived by hunting everything from rabbits to mammoth and by gathering berries and seeds. They are the distant ancestors of modern-day Native American tribes. One of their few tangible legacies, though, is the spearheads they chipped from stone, able to survive millennia of Kansas elements.

One such stone point reared its head about a hundred years ago at Twelve Mile Creek.

Twelve Mile Creek, today a small stream, runs north to south into the Smoky Hill River on the High Plains of western Kansas, about forty miles from the Colorado border. In 1895, Logan

County resident Charles Wood found fossil teeth eroding in the stream's banks at the north edge of the Smoky Hill River Valley. A nearby steep slope, cut vertically by Twelve Mile Creek, revealed a trove of prehistoric treasures. Wood contacted a party of University of Kansas paleontologists digging around the western part of the state and led department assistants Handel T. Martin and T. R. Overton to the discovery.

Martin and Overton set about extracting the fossils of thirteen bison—a now-extinct form—from a blue-gray silt "bone bed" of about ten square feet. One of the skeletons even had a fetal skeleton in its pelvis, suggesting that the kill happened in late winter or early spring, when wild animals reproduce. These were exciting discoveries in themselves during that early era of paleontology, but the real gem of the dig was a small piece of flint—a projectile point touching a shoulder blade of the largest skeleton in the bunch.

When Martin made this find, it was the first time a professional in North America had uncovered a fluted point—proof of man's presence—in connection with something so old: ten thousand years old, in fact, at a time when many archaeologists believed that humans arrived on the continent no earlier than three thousand years ago. Furthermore, it was the first discovery of a paleoindian bison kill. The bison skeleton that yielded the projectile point might have been the first bison skeleton ever mounted for public exhibition, and it's still referenced in many textbooks. But, in many ways, the paleontology community of the day failed to grasp the importance of Twelve Mile Creek.

First, the spearhead went missing.

It disappeared—was stolen, perhaps—from the University of Kansas paleontology department. It's still missing today. All that remains of the fluted point is a photograph and a simple drawing. This snafu cast doubt on the Kansas discovery linking prehistoric humans and animals, as did the paleontologists' reluctance to allow outsiders to analyze and validate their findings.

Decades later, in the 1920s, paleontologists discovered a spearhead between the ribs of a bison skeleton near Folsom, New Mexico. The skeleton was ten thousand years old, no one made off with the fluted point, and Folsom became one of the most famous archaeological sites in North America. Articles and personal letters show Twelve Mile Creek to have been influential on the excavators at Folsom, but the Kansas site's opportunity for real fame had passed.

Later analysis of the Twelve Mile Creek findings, however, proved that the discovery had been legit and the first of its kind. Radiocarbon readings dated the fossils to about 8400 B.C., more than ten thousand years ago, and ancient scrapes to the bone, covered in root marks, proved that someone had butchered the animals. Furthermore, photographs of the missing projectile point reveal it to be the appropriate style of point associated with paleoindians— information unknown to researchers at the turn of the century.

Twelve Mile Creek had even more tricks up its sleeve, though.

First, the discovered spearhead appeared to have been resharpened, thus shortening it from its original shape. A lengthened version of the point would be categorized as a "Clovis"-era projectile point, which archaeologists now know predates the shorter sort of points found at the Folsom site by a good thousand years. So, either the carbon dating was off a good deal, or the hunters were a bit behind the times in tool-making.

They were ahead of their time, though, in hunting techniques. By and large, Clovis hunters killed their prey by surrounding it and stabbing it with multiple sharp weapons. But the hunters at Twelve Mile Creek seem to have driven the bison herd over a cliff—a clever tactic thought to have been developed much later. The small area in which the skeletons were found, just ten square feet, could only hold such a number of bison if they were piled atop one another, as they would end up if plummeting from the same point. And the fossil pile's proximity to a stream channel and a steep drop leaves little doubt that the bison fell to their death.

The Twelve Mile Creek people threw archaeologists for yet another loop by decapitating their prey. The remains' detached skulls and hack marks along neck vertebrae seem to prove this, though few other paleoindian sites reveal the practice of removing bison heads.

Another important clue that Twelve Mile Creek gives us to the long-ago past: pollen, stuck in the silt that coated the bison fossils. Once analyzed, the pollen told researchers that western Kansas in 8400 B.C. was a very different place from the flat, dry expanse we know today. When paleoindians hunted and gathered, the area was moist and partially covered with the pine forests now receded to the Rocky Mountains.

Many fossils have been uncovered in Kansas, including those of toothy, forty-foot reptiles who swam the sea that covered the state more than a hundred million years ago. But arguably none has involved such controversy as the slain bison of Twelve Mile Creek.

CITY OF GOLD, SEA OF GRASS

1541

Kansas is known today for its acres and acres of golden wheat. Just plain gold, though? Not so much.

Unfortunately for Francisco Vázquez de Coronado, he didn't know as much in 1541. Coronado, the famed Spanish conquistador, staked everything on his belief that a journey north from Mexico to modern-day Kansas would yield boundless riches. He just had to get to Quivira, the city of gold.

The rumor and eventual legend of Quivira had hung over Spain for centuries, probably beginning around 1150, when seven Catholic bishops fled Spain during the Crusades. Legend had it that these bishops crossed the ocean and discovered faraway lands of immense treasures. Excitement over these rich cities flared up in 1536, when Spanish explorer Cabeza de Vaca and his companions wandered from Florida to Mexico and reported finding magnificent villages along the way. A few years later, Spain got serious about exploring the mysterious northern expanse of the New World.

Coronado, thirty years old, was charged with leading an expedition of more than three hundred Spaniards on horseback, along with about a thousand native servants and slaves. The king supplied plenty of weapons, sparkling metal armor, horses, and food, including herds of livestock that would be along for the ride. The journey began February 23, 1540, at Compostela, heading north along Mexico's western coast. With such a massive entourage, the going was slow; after a month, they had traveled three hundred miles and reached the coastal city of Culiacan. Tapped out of many of their supplies, the explorers refueled there before a select group of them, including Coronado, pushed across the Rio Sonora, into the White Mountains of modern-day New Mexico and Arizona—eighty years before the pilgrims would land at Plymouth Rock. There, in the distance, they saw a large dwelling that surely would be a city of gold.

But what they actually had found was a simple village of a few hundred Zuni tribesmen. The place was not made of sparkling towers but of flat-roofed pueblos three or four stories high, and its riches weren't metals but rather corn, beans, fowl, and salt. Coronado sent his crossbowmen and musketeers forward in attack, but the natives did not give up their home easily. Coronado, decked out in shiny armor for the occasion, himself received several blows. "They knocked me down to the ground twice with countless great stones which they threw down from above, and if I had not been protected by the very good headpiece which I wore, I think that the outcome would have been bad for me," he later wrote. The Zuni surrendered, and the Spanish army took over the village, guaranteeing food and shelter for the troops.

Despite the disappointment of finding no gold at this first battle, Coronado still had his eye on the prize. He was heartened by natives' reports of great civilizations to the east and dispatched some of his men to explore those lands. One group found the impressive Pueblo dwellings near what we now call the Pecos River, promptly kicking out the natives and commandeering food, supplies, and women for their own purposes.

Soon a native they called "the Turk," due to his dark complexion, described to them a place to the northeast called Quivira, a great kingdom full of the riches for which they'd hoped. Gold bells hung from trees there, he said, and even the water jugs were made of gold. He himself once had a golden bracelet from this land, he said. He agreed to lead the men to Quivira.

Other prisoners denied the Turk's claims, even under torture, but Coronado very much wanted to believe these latest stories of treasure. He needed something to show the king for his expedition. After a revolt among the Pueblo, he ordered the brutal massacre of hundreds of their people and was ready to move on.

Following a cold winter along the Rio Grande, Coronado moved his entire group of more than fifteen hundred Spanish soldiers and native slaves in April 1541. When they saw for the first time the Great Plains of North America, Coronado's men were astounded by the landscape—its innumerable bison, its flat expanses of grass, its nomadic tribes. One captain wrote that the bison were "the most monstrous beasts ever seen or read about. . . . I do not know what to compare them with unless it be the fish in the sea . . . because the plains were covered with them." The people, he said, "clothe themselves with cotton and the skins of cows and dress of the feathers of the fowls." Another Spaniard wrote of their complete sustenance on bison in lieu of growing corn as the southwestern tribes did: "with the skins they make their houses, with the skins they clothe and shoe themselves, of the skins they make rope, and also of the wool; from the sinews they make thread . . . from the bones they make awls; the dung serves them for wood . . . the stomachs serve them for pitchers and vessels from which they drink; they live on the flesh; they sometimes eat it half roasted and warmed over the dung, at other times raw; seizing it with their fingers, they pull it out with one hand and with a flint knife in the other they cut off mouthfuls . . . they drink the blood just as it leaves the cows . . . they have no other means of livelihood." Coronado described the plains as "so vast that I did not find the limit anywhere that I went, although I traveled over them for more than 300 leagues."

But after traveling east, the Turk began to lead them into a confusing ocean of grass. Coronado wrote, "I traveled five days more as the guides wished to lead me, until I reached some plains, with no more landmarks than as if we had been swallowed up in the sea because there was not a stone, nor a bit of rising ground, nor a tree, nor a shrub nor anything to go by." Another chronicler marveled at the sheer flatness of the land: "The country is so level that men became lost when they went off half a league. One horseman was lost, who never reappeared, and two horses, all saddled and bridled, which they never saw again. No track was left of where they went." They were somewhere in northern Texas, pummeled by the area's powerful springtime thunderstorms. "The hail broke many tents, and battered many helmets, and wounded many of the horses, and broke all the crockery of the army," one conquistador wrote. More importantly, the group was utterly lost, in a sea of grass. This may have been the Turk's goal.

The Spanish eventually encountered a nomadic Teya tribe, who insisted that there was no "city of gold," but Coronado pressed north with about thirty of his best men—and the Turk.

After more than a month traversing the plains, crossing the Texas and Oklahoma panhandles, Coronado crossed "the river Quivira"— the Arkansas River—somewhere near Dodge City. Soon they found the Quivira people, now known as the Wichita. Their village was smack in the middle of Kansas, around today's Rice County, and utterly devoid of gold. The straw huts where he had imagined walls of gold finally crushed Coronado's faith in a mythical kingdom. His conquistadors tortured the Turk into confessing that he had led them astray intentionally, in an attempt to free the Pueblo people at the Pecos River. He was strangled to death.

The Spanish stayed with the Quivira for some time before returning to earlier posts, being sure along the way to raise a cross into which was chiseled Coronado's name. This cross appears to be lost to time, though Spanish artifacts such as chain mail have been found in Kansas and across the plains. (In 1886 a Kansas man discovered a rusted sword blade in central Kansas near Cimarron; it was inscribed with the words "No me saques sin razon; no me enbaines sin honor," a common inscription for Spanish swords meaning "Draw me not without reason; sheath me not without honor." A hundred years later, though, experts would date the sword to the 1700s, far too late to have belonged to Coronado's men.)

During the winter of 1541–1542, his ambitions defeated, Coronado was badly trampled by his own horse during a frivolous race. One of his captains reported that, during Coronado's recovery, the general "recollected what a scientific friend of his in Salamanca had told him, that he would become a powerful lord in distant lands, and that he would have a fall from which he would never be able to recover. This expectation of death made him desire to return and die where he had a wife and children."

In April 1542, his expedition having covered four thousand miles without finding any gold, Coronado left America.

INDIAN REMOVAL

1831

The people of the Delaware tribe were bone-thin and freezing in their new land, a windy plain that looked and smelled different than their home in the east. This place, which soon would be called Kansas, was flatter than the places they had known, with no dense forests, no hills or trees to break the winter wind. The Delaware never wanted to come here. The United States government had forced them to move—again.

As white settlers expanded south and west from their colonial regions, they repeatedly encountered tribes of native people whose presence they found cumbersome to development. In the 1700s, the Delaware and other northeastern tribes were forced south to make room for white expansion. Then, in 1830, President Andrew Jackson pushed the Indian Removal Act into law, allowing for even more aggressive federal action against native peoples. William Clark, the superintendent of Indian affairs and former explorer of Lewis and Clark fame, had paved the way for the Delaware's removal earlier that year, as he outlined in a letter to Secretary of War John Eaton in February 1830.

I take the liberty of enclosing a letter or talk receaved a few days agoe from Chief Anderson of the Delaware Nation of Indians, and his Captains, on the Subject of exchanging Their lands within the State, for Lands on the Kanzas River, by which it appears they are anxious to effectly reducing the Terms on which they were willing to exchange two years agoe except the additional Annuity and paying their Traders their demands, is such as they will necessarily require to enable them to progress with any certainty of success on lands which is contemplated for them to settle upon.

So, soon after the Indian Removal Act became law, the Delaware found themselves moved once more—this time, pushed west toward what is now Kansas. Yanked from their stores of food and supplies, the tribe now relied on the U.S. government for sustenance, with an "Indian agent" serving as a liaison.

One agent, Richard Cummins, met the Delaware in late 1830 as they passed through Missouri en route to the Kansas River. As winter was settling in, the tribe's leaders demanded the provisions and annuity payments that their people had been promised. Cummins relayed this to his boss, William Clark. In a letter dated December 3, 1830, Cummins asks Clark whether he should deliver food and clothing to the four hundred Delaware—among them, women, children, and elderly—nearing their new home.

"The Chiefs demand of me their provisions as provided for in their Treaty, and say it was to be delivered to them on their land, if it was your intention or wish that I should furnish them there provisions on their land I wish you to instruct me to that effect, I have told them that their Treaty was not yet ratified, and that no Appropriation was made to carry it into effect," Cummins wrote.

Cummins's efforts did nothing to hasten assistance to the tribe, though. The Delaware would receive little help in the difficult business of moving hundreds of people and horses across the country in the bitter cold. The tribe reached its destination amid an exceptionally harsh winter and continued to wait for the help. Repeatedly, they were told that their treaty with the U.S. government hadn't been ratified yet—a hang-up they found curious, considering that white settlers had seized their land in the east even before they left for Kansas. Cummins watched as the Delaware starved and froze, following orders by delivering the bare minimum of food and supplies. Still, troubled by the suffering he witnessed over the course of the winter, Cummins in April wrote another letter to Clark.

> *Shawanee and Delaware Agency*
> *Genl. William Clark*
> *2d April 1831*
> *Sup't of Indian Aff's*
> *Sir,*
> *I have furnished the Delawares with as much provisions only as was actually needful to keep them from suffering, which I had To transport to them, when they came last fall their horses were poor, oweing [owing] to the very extreme Hardness of the winter, the Indians generally as weel [well] as the Delawares lost most all their horses. They have none fit for service, a great many of the Indians, are in a suffering condition Owing chiefly to the unusual hardness of the winter. I believed it to be my duty to have some provisions Waggoned to them, particularly, to the Delawares Chief Anderson & his counsel*

men says that it was understood last fall on White river
that the supplementary article to their treaty was rati-
fied, That immediately the white people moved in among
Them and took possession of their farms. Commenced
seeding their fields and selling whiskey to his people so
that he was compelled to move. I have also furnished
that half of the, Weas, that have been in the Mississippi
swamps, for some time past with Two waggon loads of
Corn and pork. They came and joined their, Nation
on their Land this spring, in a starving condition, their
Friends were unable to help them many of whom I was
informed by the trader divided their corn with their
horses as long as they had an ear, they are now trying to
work but their diet is so weak, they are not able to do
much. I think the past winter, will learn the Indians in
future to be more provident. They stand much in need of
provisions, I would like to receive some instructions from
You on the subject of furnishing them.
Respectfully Your Most
Obedt. Servt.
Richd. W. Cummins

The Delawares' situation was hardly unique. During the period of "Indian removal," up to ten thousand Native Americans and more than thirty tribes—including the Wea, from New York, whom Cummins also mentions—were relocated to the territory that would become Kansas. These tribes, which also included the Ottawa, Miami, Cayuga, Seneca, Muncie, Wyandot, Delaware, and Shawnee, weren't entering vacant lands. Kansas had been occupied by the Kanza and Pawnee tribes for centuries. Such sudden condensing of peoples with very different languages and cultures created additional strains beyond the need for food and supplies. Conflicts over resources and territory erupted among tribes. Meanwhile, many like the Delaware had to fight for the U.S. government to keep its promises of supplies or, perhaps more importantly, freedoms. Despite their many sacrifices and the promises of the government, they were hard-pressed to keep white settlers from entering their new land. The Trade and Intercourse Acts were meant to prohibit such settlement, as well as to keep whites from selling whiskey and weapons to Native Americans or trading with them in general. But these laws were largely disregarded and, as Kansas moved toward statehood with the Kansas-Nebraska Act of 1854, it was clear that Native Americans would be forced to move yet again.

In about thirty years, the Delaware would be moved again, this time south to present-day Oklahoma.

THE POTTAWATOMIE MASSACRE

1856

The year 1856 was a wild one in Kansas.

The territory, newly settled by whites but not yet an official state, had become a battleground over the question of slavery. The 1854 passing of the Kansas-Nebraska Act had repealed the Missouri Compromise of 1820 and allowed for slavery above the 36' 30" line, the latitudinal mark that fell just past Kansas's southern border. Popular sovereignty was to decide whether Kansas—not quite north and not quite south—would be a slave state or a free state. Kansas was brimming with abolitionist settlers; some morally objected to slavery, while others were motivated by their wish to live in an all-white community of homesteaders, rather than a landscape dotted with plantations and blacks. However, the territory was saddled next to the slave state of Missouri, ensuring that Kansas would have a difficult and bloody time carving out its identity.

Zealots on both sides of the fight traveled to Kansas from the north and south to leave their mark; some towns, such as Atchison and Leavenworth, were pro-slavery, while others, such as Lawrence and Topeka, were free-staters. By 1856, skirmishes, town raids, and individual killings over slavery had turned the eyes of the nation on Kansas. When Governor Wilson Shannon resigned from office that summer, he remarked, "Govern Kansas! . . . You might as well attempt to govern the devil in hell."

This period of "Bleeding Kansas" reached a fever pitch with the destruction of Lawrence, an abolitionist stronghold, on May 21, 1856. It was a piercing victory for the pro-slavery factions; the people and buildings of Lawrence lay dead and burning, and most of the offending "Border Ruffians" from Missouri had escaped unscathed. While the people of Lawrence were still reeling, one man thirsted for vengeance.

John Brown was a New England man, but in 1855 he had joined five of his sons homesteading in Kansas Territory. The men built a log cabin called "Brown's Station" along Pottawatomie Creek, where they hoarded weapons, traded harsh words with their pro-slavery neighbors, and maintained hopes to bring Kansas into the Union as a free state. Brown's sons and their friends, led by John Jr., called themselves the Pottawatomie Rifles.

Upon hearing that Lawrence would be attacked, the Rifles and the elder Brown assembled and began their journey to defend the town. Along the way, they received word that the town already had burned. Brown boiled with indignation over the ease with which the Ruffians had destroyed unsuspecting Lawrence in the early morning hours. En route to Lawrence, he heard of yet another offense to his cause—the brutal beating of abolitionist U.S. senator Charles Sumner on the Senate floor by a southern congressman, following Sumner's passionate speech entitled "The Crime Against Kansas." By then, Brown was seeing red. While the Pottawatomie Rifles debated what to do next, he had his own plan.

Brown told Rifle member James Townsley, who happened to have a wagon with him, that he'd received news of unrest back at

Pottawatomie Creek. Would Townsley take him and his boys back, so that they might keep watch over their home? Townsley agreed, setting out the afternoon of the 23rd with John Sr. and his sons Frederick, Owen, Watson, and Oliver, as well as Brown's son-in-law and another militiaman. A couple miles from home, the group turned off the road to camp for the night. That evening, John Brown finally made his real plans known. He asked Townsley to take the group several miles up the creek, to the area where he lived, and point out the homes of each pro-slavery man. Then, Brown said, they would make a murderous sweep of all the homes. Townsley refused, suggesting that they fight pro-slavery leaders in open fields at the nearby capital of Lecompton rather than murder men in their own homes. But Brown was undeterred. The next night, May 24th, he and his group set out with swords and rifles.

Brown and four others first knocked on the door of the James Doyle residence while Townsley and the rest fought off an attack dog. When Doyle and two of his sons came out of the house, Brown shot the elder Doyle in the forehead. It was the only shot the group would fire, favoring instead the quiet of their swords so as not to alarm neighbors. Brown's two youngest sons stabbed the Doyle sons to death; one managed to get away, dripping blood as he ran, but ultimately was cut down.

Next, they knocked on the door of the Allen Wilkinson residence; Wilkinson was marched south of the house and killed with a short sword by one of Brown's sons.

The band then crossed the Pottawatomie to reach the home of Henry Sherman, known as Dutch Henry, a pro-slavery militant. Dutch Henry wasn't home, though, so Brown's men instead killed his brother, William Sherman, with swords and left him lying in the road.

After midnight, five men were dead. The number would have been higher, had Brown had his way. Several pro-slavery men marked by Brown were not found, including George Wilson, probate judge of Anderson County, who had been attempting to drive free-staters out of the Territory. According to Townsley, Brown said "that the Pro-slavery party must be terrified and that it was better that a score of bad men should die than that one man who came here to make Kansas a free State should be driven out."

Brown and his company rejoined John Jr. and the Pottawatomie Rifles the next night; John Jr., presumably unnerved by his father's actions, resigned from his position as captain of the militia and kept watch over the renegade group in his cabin and his brother Jason's cabin. After several days of lying low, the men received word that John Brown was being hunted. The group left on horseback, hiding in forests and strengthening their numbers with more free-staters. John Jr. and Jason stayed behind and were taken prisoner by Henry Pate, a pro-slavery fighter who had participated in the raid on Lawrence.

Hearing of his sons' capture, Brown and his band, now thirty strong, started toward Black Jack Point, where Pate reportedly was camped. When the group neared the camp on June 2, seven men remained with the horses while the rest assailed Pate and his men, quickly cornering them in a ravine and fighting until Pate surrendered three hours later, ultimately freeing Brown's sons. This, the Battle of Black Jack, is considered by many to be the unofficial first battle of the Civil War. Indeed, the entire Bleeding Kansas period—which escalated tensions across the country and killed approximately fifty-five people—set the stage for the war between North and South.

Brown himself kept his finger on the national pulse toward war, spending the years following the Battle of Black Jack devising a massive uprising against the federal government and its slavery-enabling laws. In 1859, he led a siege on the U.S. Armory and Arsenal at Harpers Ferry, Virginia, and attempted to invoke a slave revolt. The mission failed, and Brown was hanged.

His death inspired great sentiment within the anti-slavery movement and made him something of a martyr. In an 1881 speech, scholar and former slave Frederick Douglass delivered a speech at Harper's Ferry, stating, "Did John Brown fail? John Brown began the war that ended American slavery and made this a free Republic." By 1910, however, when former president Theodore Roosevelt gave a speech in Kansas to commemorate a John Brown memorial, leading thinkers such as Roosevelt and William Allen White saw Brown as a misguided extremist. When in 1941 the nationally known Kansas painter John Steuart Curry painted in the state capitol a mural of a wild-faced Brown wielding a Bible and a rifle, much controversy ensued; many Kansans objected to the idea that Brown might represent the people and heart of their state.

QUANTRILL'S RAID

1863

Twenty-six-year-old Kate Riggs awoke to the sound of large fire-crackers. That's what she thought she heard, anyway, groggy and startled at dawn. Her husband, Samuel, ran to the window, open to the August air, and saw armed men running across the street near the heart of Lawrence. He turned to his wife.

"Quantrill's band, as sure as you live," he said.

Rumors had begun circulating in July that renegade Confederate soldier William Quantrill was planning a major attack on Lawrence, an anti-slavery stronghold of three thousand people, about a hundred miles from the Kansas-Missouri border. Samuel, a twenty-eight-year-old attorney, had particular concern for his safety; he had prosecuted Quantrill three years earlier, in 1860, for burglary, larceny, arson, and kidnapping. Samuel had tried the case under the name "Charley Hart," to avoid retribution by Quantrill and his gang—pro-slavery Missourians known for their guerilla tactics against Kansas abolitionists in the midst of the Civil War. Townspeople had taken watch-posts about town; for his part,

Samuel stood guard with a musket near his stone house on the 700 block of Rhode Island Street.

But weeks passed, the town relaxed, and Riggs's musket rested in the dining room.

Now, at 5:00 a.m. on August 21, 1863, Quantrill and his men had caught the town of Lawrence off-guard.

Kate ran to get dressed when she saw through the window the first of the many horrors she would witness that day.

A man was riding toward the back gate. Another man, lying in the grass, said, "You have shot me." The man on horseback responded by dismounting and shooting the wounded man twice more.

At that moment, scenes such as this were playing out all over town, as about four hundred of Quantrill's men rode the streets of Lawrence, shooting men and boys, looting businesses, robbing families, setting fire to nearly every structure they passed. The Riggs could see the Lewis house next door burning and smoke billowing from the Lowe house across the street while raiders made off with various goods.

Kate slowly moved from sight and ran to the dining room for the musket. She hid it behind the potato bin in the cellar. Meanwhile, Samuel, believing he would be taken prisoner, hid fifty dollars and a gold watch in the attic for his wife.

But Kate marched to the attic herself, putting the money in her pocket and the watch around her neck. If they took him prisoner, she informed her husband, she was going with him.

Kate and Samuel decided to check on their neighbors. Samuel went next door to help Mrs. Lewis search for salvageable belongings among the charred remains of her home, while Kate went across the street to find Mr. Lowe trying to save his house from a fire Quantrill's men had started with mattresses and dresses.

"Oh, Mrs. Riggs, isn't this a great day?" said the Lowes' young son. Kate, fearing that her husband was a marked man, warned Mrs. Lowe not to speak the Riggs name.

More of Quantrill's men rode past demanding money and valuables, and Samuel overheard their plans to burn every house in town. So he and Kate went back to their house to bundle up a few silk dresses and blankets that might be thrown out the window in case of a fire. Kate was on her way to roll a few items into their horse-hair mattress when she saw through the window another neighbor, Mr. Burt, being approached by a gruff man on a large horse. Burt spread his hands to signal that he had given all his money and belongings already. The man shot Mr. Burt in the chest.

Kate called to her husband to come inside, but it was too late. The man with the big horse was talking to Samuel at their front gate. Kate watched as he handed over the $4.50 in his pocket. Just as she reached her husband's side, the man on the horse turned his revolver on Samuel.

"Well, you are a damned black Republican anyhow," the man said and pulled the trigger.

But the gun did not fire. Samuel took the instant to lunge at the man. Unable to pry the gun from the man's hands, though, Samuel ran across the street to take cover behind the Lowe house as the man shouted curses and threats and turned his horse in Samuel's direction.

Without thinking, Kate leapt toward the horse and seized its bridle just as it took off. Onlookers screamed at the spectacle, but the man pushed his horse forward, hell-bent on murdering Kate's husband. Samuel heard the ruckus and turned to see his wife running alongside his assailant's horse, using her weight to direct it away from Samuel. The man, the horse, and Kate struggled up Rhode Island Street into open prairie until the man finally got the horse turned around; he took the horse across a wood pile, all the while dragging Kate, her dark hair in the wind. They finally stopped at the smoldering Rollins residence, to which Samuel had darted.

Spotting Samuel, the man aimed his revolver. Kate yanked the horse around to unsettle the man's aim, but he turned on the horse and fired, and then raised his gun to strike Kate's hands. She released the bridle and ran before he could strike her.

"Where did that man go?" the man demanded of Mrs. Rollins, struggling to see through the thick smoke that hid Samuel.

"I don't know," she said.

Kate didn't know, either, and feared he might have come upon some other danger.

Once the horseman had gone, the other men of the street came from their hiding places. Mr. Rollins informed Kate that her husband had hid in the corn crib at the edge of the Riggs property. She checked for any of Quantrill's men, went to the corncrib and urged Samuel to make a break for the house while he could.

Not long after Samuel ran to the house, another man found Kate in their yard and asked for her husband, but she played dumb. Then, one of Kate's friends came rushing to her—she had heard that Samuel was dead. (In fact, a different Samuel Riggs had been killed.)

By then, four hours had passed since the invasion, and Lawrence was a different place. The firing had stopped, but the air was filled with cries of agony; 180 people were dead and most of the town was on fire, the main commercial strip of Massachusetts Street a veritable wall of flames. The economic blow to the town was severe, with one newspaper estimating the property losses at $2 million, the equivalent of more than $50 million in 2009.

Farmers began riding into town with shotguns and food, to help however they might. Kate heard through the grapevine that a group of them had intercepted her husband's would-be murderer; they meant to haul the captive to Lawrence, but when he bragged of killing thirteen men in Lawrence, they shot him.

Being among the more fortunate households that day, Kate and Samuel spent the rest of the day doing their best to feed and clothe the many hungry, newly homeless Lawrencians now wandering the streets. They consoled their many friends who had lost husbands, brothers, and sons—including Mrs. Lowe, whose husband died trying to rescue two men who had hidden in a well ultimately overtaken by a nearby house fire.

The weekend was spent digging graves and feeding the hungry. Most people hadn't slept much in three days, and a sense of fear lingered about the traumatized town. By Sunday night, an eerie cold front—unheard of for August in Kansas—had blown in, and a rumor was circling that Quantrill's gang would return. So the surviving men gathered on Massachusetts Street with torches and guns, and women were ferried to the north side of the Kansas River for their safety.

Not Kate, though.

She defied her husband, friends, and even a sheriff in refusing to board the ferry. She would later write to her grandchildren, "I had made up my mind not to go in any case, as your grandfather was the only one belonging to me and I was not going to put the river between us."

The fear proved unfounded, as Quantrill's band did not return. But fear gave way to anger. Brigadier General Thomas Ewing ordered the evacuation of Missouri counties near the border, and Union troops destroyed the area in retaliation for what would be known as the Lawrence Massacre, or Quantrill's Raid.

EXODUSTERS

1877

Before the town of Nicodemus even existed, pamphlets and posters enticed Lexington, Kentucky, blacks with the claim, "The Largest Colored Colony in America."

In the decade or so since the Civil War's end, southern blacks had endured the trials of Reconstruction, a period in which poverty and racism continued to shackle newly "freed" slaves despite federal occupation of the area. Lacking education, skills, or legal protections to navigate the free world, many continued to work for their old masters as sharecroppers. By 1877, they were willing to leave their longtime home in the South for a place that promised land ownership, cheap living, freedom, and adventure. Western Kansas, a vast swath of prairie grass far beyond the Mississippi River, was just such a place.

The promises came from two men: W. H. Smith, a black minister from Kentucky, and W. R. Hill, a white land developer from Indiana. In 1877 they joined forces on 161 acres of Graham County, population 75, to form the Nicodemus Town Company—named for the legendary slave who purchased his own freedom. Reverend Smith assumed the role of president, and Hill became treasurer. They set out to foster a truly free, all-black community, and make a buck in the process.

The first brave settler, Reverend Simon P. Roundtree, arrived in June, soon followed by Smith's daughter and her husband, Zack Fletcher, who became the secretary of Nicodemus. The town's inception was extremely humble; so few trees were to be found on the western Kansas landscape that the settlers lacked timber for building, and were forced to make their homes in earthen dugouts on the prairie.

This didn't stop Smith and Hill from exaggerating the resources of their new town to black would-be settlers. A wealth of animals to hunt! Horses to be tamed! Land to be homesteaded! The fliers they distributed to southern blacks, mostly in Kentucky and Tennessee, called the area "the Great Solomon Valley" and extolled a rich, fertile landscape quite different from the dry, windswept plain that awaited settlers. But former slaves who were starving and oppressed in war-ravaged states didn't take much convincing. Plus, many associated Kansas with the famous abolitionist John Brown and with its bloody struggle to finally enter the union as a free state.

A black man from Louisiana, S. L. Johnson, wrote a letter to Kansas governor John St. John in 1879 demonstrating the great esteem in which southern blacks held the place. "I am anxious to reach your state," he wrote, "because of the sacredness of her soil washed by the blood of humanitarians for the cause of freedom." (St. John gave a speech welcoming the southern blacks, though he later tempered such comments, perhaps due to political pressure from whites who were wary of Nicodemus and similar settlements.)

Reverend Roundtree and a black carpenter named Singleton helped with the promotion cause, the latter earning the name "Moses of the Colored Exodus" for leading blacks from the south to Nicodemus. In the late summer of 1877, more than three hundred southern black "Exodusters" emerged from the nearest train station, in Ellis, and walked fifty-five miles to their promised land; within weeks came the first birth of a black child in the county to Henry Williams and his wife. Nearly another hundred settlers followed in the next two years.

They weren't entirely thrilled with what they found.

One woman, Willianna Hickman, explained her first impression of the town in 1878.

"When we got in sight of Nicodemus, the men shouted, 'there is Nicodemus!' Being very sick, I hailed this news with gladness. I looked with all the eyes I had. 'Where is Nicodemus? I don't see it.' My Husband pointed out various smokes coming out of the ground and said, 'That is Nicodemus.' The families lived in dugouts. . . . The scenery was not at all inviting, and I began to cry."

People lived "like prairie dogs," she said, digging holes in the earth along the Solomon River for shelter. The dry, flat stretch of tall, yellow grass and limestone earth was a shock to those who had spent their lives in the green, forested hills of the South. Lacking tools, food, planting seeds, and money, some returned to their homes in the South. Others stayed, including Reverend Daniel Hickman and his wife Willianna, of Kentucky, who founded the First Baptist Church in a sod structure.

Their first attempts at growing crops offered little return, owing to the hard ground and difficult climate. During the first hard winter, some black settlers were forced to turn to the Osage Indians for food and assistance.

Nonetheless, through years of hard work, the Exodusters turned their new home into a successful agricultural economy. Favorable weather in the mid-1880s resulted in high yields for their wheat and other crops; amid this prosperity, one county resident, Thomas Johnson, managed to grow his land ownership to one thousand acres.

The mid-1880s boom in Nicodemus spread beyond the fields. Black businessmen thrived alongside white business owners, and stone structures replaced dugout homes. Thirty new buildings went up in 1886. The sodden Baptist church was replaced with a stone sanctuary. The Fletcher-Switzer House, constructed in 1880, provided a post office, hotel, stable, and school, all launched primarily by Zack and Jenny Fletcher, the town founder's daughter. They filled the roles of postmaster and postmistress, hotel-stable owner and schoolteacher. In addition, Jenny helped establish the African Methodist Episcopal Church, which began in an earth structure in 1879 but graduated to a limestone building in 1885.

Soon, Nicodemus was nearly five hundred strong, with a bank, newspaper, drugstore, three general stores, two hotels, and three churches—and miles of fields beyond its commercial center. By the late 1880s, just a decade after its inception, it boasted more stores and churches, pharmacies, barbershops, a second newspaper, an ice cream parlor, and its own baseball team and band. Resident Edward P. McCabe became the first African American to hold a major state office in Kansas, serving two terms as state auditor, from 1883 to 1887.

The *Nicodemus Cyclone* celebrated the triumphs of former slaves in a June 15, 1886, commentary: "Nicodemus . . . was originally settled by the colored race, and by their patience and untiring energy have succeeded in gaining a grand, glorious victory over nature and the elements, and what used to be the Great American Desert now blooms with waving grain."

Soon, Nicodemus received word that the Missouri Pacific and the Union Pacific railroads might lay tracks through town as they expanded westward. The town approved thousands of dollars in bonds to attract the companies, but both bypassed the town. Union Pacific instead laid tracks six miles away, south of the Solomon River.

This turn of events threatened disaster for Nicodemus, as many businesses talked of making the short move to the railroad to boost business. The *Nicodemus Cyclone* warned against such actions on September 7, 1888:

> *We are sorry to see several of our business men mak-*
> *ing preparations to move to the proposed new town.*
> *We consider this a very unwise move and one they*
> *will regret. With a thickly settled surrounding, already*
> *established in business and as reliably informed in*
> *the extension on the Stockton road in the near future,*
> *Nicodemus and her business men have nothing to cause*
> *them alarm. For every one that goes now we will get*
> *ten wide awake men next spring. Don't get frightened*
> *hold on to your property and be ready to enjoy the real*
> *boom that will surely come.*

But the businesses moved anyway, establishing a camp south of the river that later would be known as the town of Bogue. Coupled with the economic depression of the 1890s, it was a blow that knocked Nicodemus from its brief period of prosperity. The following decades marked a long decline, as more and more families left their struggling town. The Dust Bowl and Great Depression wreaked further havoc on local agriculture, and by 1935 Nicodemus was down to just seventy-five inhabitants.

Unlike other black settlements west of the Mississippi, though, the town would survive. In 2009, Nicodemus was home to twenty people and was the only remaining town in the West founded by former slaves. Locals and the town's descendants have taken great care to continue to honor the great achievements of Nicodemus's settlers, and the town was named a National Historic Site in 1996.

DODGING PROHIBITION

1880

Unlike whiskey and water, Dodge City and Prohibition just didn't mix.

When Kansas became the first state in the union to ban alcohol in its constitution in 1880, the decree fell on deaf ears in the country's most famous Wild West town.

"The open saloon shall be and is hereby forever prohibited," read Article 15 of the state constitution. Tell gunslingers in dusty saloons not to drink whiskey? You might as well tell grass not to grow on the prairie.

A Hays City reporter wrote of Dodge City's newspapers in 1877, "Every other item is description of how some drunken rowdy nearly beat the life out of his mistress, or somebody else's mistress; the police court report often fills columns, and even the decent portion of the community have become so accustomed to the fearful state of affairs that they regard a good stand-up fight . . . a joke rather than a disgrace."

Surely the beer taps in Dodge City could not be turned off.

But Prohibitionist sentiment had swept the state—thirty-nine years before the federal government banned alcohol. As Kansas newspaper editor William Allen White wrote, "Things start in Kansas that finish in history." Abolition, prohibition, public health regulations—indeed, the state was at the forefront of these and other movements, often thanks to the New England moralists who had settled in Kansas to fight for a free state in the 1850s. Still, such moralism was often just a public display. "Kansans will vote dry so long as they can stagger to the polls," one writer commented. Citizens drank moonshine in their own living rooms but frowned on bastions of sin like Dodge City. Even the tamer residents of Dodge felt moved to champion Prohibition in the hopes of cleaning up their infamous town.

But liquor license revenues were the economic lifeblood of Dodge, and mayor Jim Kelley did not jump at the chance to implement the new state law. Nor did he do much in the way of curtailing the general lawlessness on the streets. Citizens forced him from office and made way for a new mayor, Alonzo Webster. A Civil War vet and conservative businessman, no-nonsense Webster let it be known that "thieves, thugs, confidence men, and persons without visible means of support" would not be tolerated—a promise he made good on not long after taking office, when he ran famous outlaw Bat Masterson out of town—and that policemen, wearing newly assigned blue uniforms, would actually enforce the law, including Prohibition. Prostitutes and gamblers were fined, as were the newly illegal saloons still slinging drinks. Webster didn't buy into radical anti-drinking sentiment of the times, and his approach—just enough penalty to keep the outlaws on their toes, while alcohol was served up anyway—got him re-elected without opposition. Meanwhile, the fall 1881 election of a county sheriff whose sympathies lay with moonshiners sealed the deal: No one would really be cleaning up Dodge City any time soon. Rumors circulated that two city councilors wanted to temper gambling and prostitution; one didn't make it past the 1882 election. County attorney Mike Sutton wouldn't pursue legal action against boozers, saying it was pointless: "I shall probably take no action in the matter, because every officer in the county whose duty it will be to help me enforce the law are themselves openly and avowedly against its enforcement, and can furnish me no aid, and I know I have no moral backing."

Governor John St. John, perhaps seeking votes in the 1882 election or perhaps motivated by memories of his alcoholic father, seized the issue, amping up state surveillance of communities such as Dodge. "It seems to me, if drunkenness and crime are necessary to the growth of any city that the quicker the city can stop growing the better, if it depends on such influences for its prosperity," St. John wrote in an 1880 letter to newspaper editor George Martin.

An 1882 *New York Times* editorial criticized St. John's motives and cast doubt on the sincerity of the Kansas Prohibition movement as a whole, noting that the amendment passed ninety-two thousand to eighty-four thousand, while twenty thousand ballots in the same election did not vote on the proposition at all.

> *It will be observed that actual sentiment of the State on this proposition is still in doubt. The succeeding legislature, many members of which were not temperance men in any sense of the word, sought to make the law putting the amendment in force as obnoxious as possible. So after all the talk that has been had in regard to this measure, it is safe to say that prohibition does not prohibit. Right here in Topeka 30 or 40 saloons are open day and night, and it is just as easy to get a glass of whisky or beer in Topeka as at any time of the past. So it is in a large number of towns throughout the State, and when the Governor or*

*anybody else claims that the amendment is enforced in the
State they state that which is not true. The law is openly
violated in a hundred towns in the State every hour in
the day, and the whole prohibition scheme is the greatest
farce ever enacted by an intelligent people anywhere on
earth. . . . The truth is that Governor St. John aspires to
be President of the United States, and seeks to ride into
that important position on the prohibition hobby. Your
readers may think this a wild scheme, but many so-called
temperance journals throughout the country have already
mentioned him in connection with this position.*

Indeed, St. John would run as a Prohibition Party candidate
for president in 1884, losing to Grover Cleveland. But in the years
prior, he was consumed with the cause of "drying up" places like
Dodge. He wasn't alone. In May of 1882, the Kansas lodge of the
Good Templars set up a chapter in Dodge City from which to
affect moral influence. Nicholas Klaine, the owner of the *Dodge
City Times,* joined the movement, at least publicly. And the Santa
Fe railroad threatened to revoke Dodge's place as a major rail-
way hub—and, thus, cattle-shipping point—if the place didn't
straighten up.

Alarmed, the city agreed to close all businesses on Sundays, ban
music even in dance houses, and limit gambling to back rooms far
from sight. All of the above were routinely violated, but the official
compromise was a victory for radical reformists.

In 1883, when Dodge City papers were claiming that Prohibition had calmed the town, the rest of the state still targeted the
town as a scourge. The *Medicine Lodge Cresset* wrote, "After the last
distributor of the gospel flees with his family and household goods

to the mountains, a blizzard or a storm of hailstones and coals of fire will annihilate the town."

Dodge City businessmen, for their part, were getting fed up with the attacks and resolved among themselves to stop rolling over. David "Mysterious Dave" Mather bought part of Opera House on Front Street, planning to make the place a dance house. The city council promptly passed an ordinance outlawing dance houses. Meanwhile, a dance hall farther from the city center—and conveniently owned by assistant city marshal Thomas Nixon—was allowed to keep operating.

Mysterious Dave responded by lowering the Opera House's beer price to five cents per glass, less than half the going rate. This move succeeded in draining business from Nixon's joint; he, in turn, pressured local beer distributors to stop delivering to the Opera House.

Tensions between the men escalated. On July 18, 1884, Nixon fired an errant shot at Mysterious Dave. Three nights later, Dave shot Nixon four times, killing him.

Normally, Dave would have been hanged. But local officials were so pleased that Dave had rid them of an anti-reformer in their midst, he won an acquittal.

It was becoming clear that not even the state could stomp out the wild fires of Dodge City's cowboys, outlaws, and whiskey-lovers. In 1885, mayor Robert Wright wrote to governor John Martin, pleading for the state to let his city be:

> You must recolect [sic] that our situation is diferent
> [sic] from that of other Towns in the Eastern part of the
> State, which have always enjoyed the benefits of churches,
> schools & other civilizing influences. We have always
> been a frontier Town, where the wild & reckless sons of

*the Plains have congregated, their influences are still felt
here, but we are rapidly overcoming them, let us alone
& we will work out our salvation in due season. I flatter
myself that I know how to handle the boys, they cannot be
driven. . . . Please do not borrow trouble Governor about
the conduct or management of Dodge City.*

Eventually, alcohol won out. Prohibition was repealed at the federal level in 1933, and most states followed suit, if only by calling off enforcement of anti-drinking laws. In Kansas, Prohibition laws remained on the books, and for decades bars and restaurants officially adopted "private club" status to circumvent the "open saloon law." Finally, in 1987, 107 years after the state banned alcohol, the Kansas Constitution was amended to allow for the purchase of liquor by the drink.

THE *FARMER'S WIFE*

1890–1894

In 1859, Clarina Nichols made a bold proposition: Give Kansas women the right to vote.

She lobbied the Wyandotte Constitutional Convention, which was shaping the all-important document for the soon-to-be state of Kansas, to cut the word "male" from the suffrage clause of the Kansas Constitution. It was a bold move in a time when women had few rights and were, in many regards, the property of their fathers or husbands. Her best efforts at suffrage failed, but she did secure within the new constitution the right for women to vote in school-district elections, to obtain and own property, and to have custody of children equal to that of the father's—all rights largely unheard of throughout the United States. Nichols had left her mark, and the state had sealed its place at the forefront of the movement toward women's suffrage. When the University of Kansas opened in 1864, it was the first university in the country to "receive both men and women on an equal basis." The flame for women's equality had been lit among Kansans and would continue to burn brightly.

While a losing battle for women's suffrage was being waged at the 1867 New York Constitutional Convention, politician Sam Wood, activist Lucy Stone, and her husband, Henry Browne Blackwell, descended upon Kansas, hoping to seize populist sentiment and turn the tides for disenfranchised women. Wood was elected to the Kansas senate, and soon the state would have the first state legislature to propose women's suffrage at the constitutional level.

The Equal Rights Association campaigned furiously for this and another measure for black suffrage to be voted on in the fall general election: speeches, pamphlets, female volunteers with signs, Lucy Stone lecturing up and down the state. Famed New York suffragists Elizabeth Cady Stanton and Susan B. Anthony joined the fight on Kansas soil in September. But the opposition was fierce, and the measures for both women's and black suffrage failed, the former receiving 9,010 votes for the amendment and 19,857 votes against it.

The loss was a hard one. Stanton later wrote in *History of Woman Suffrage,* "There never was a more hopeful interest concentrated on the legislation of any single state, than when Kansas submitted the two propositions to her people to take the words 'white' and 'male' from her constitution."

Stanton and Anthony responded to this latest blow, in part, by creating a newspaper from which to espouse their views. In Kansas, they met George Francis Train, who would financially back the publication. The first issue of the weekly paper the *Revolution* was published in January 1868.

The *Revolution* and other national publications would rally for women's rights for decades, but as the twentieth century approached, more and more small, local suffragist journals sprouted across the countryside, reflecting the massive swell of the Populist Party, which supported suffrage for all and inspired workers' uprisings throughout the land. And nowhere did the populist movement and the cry for suffrage resound more clearly than in Kansas.

In a political and social climate hostile toward the idea that women might think and act on an equal playing field with men, publications arguing for women's rights were vital. With no televisions, computers, or radios, American citizens learned about the world beyond their own experience through nothing more than the printed word and conversation. Journals extolling the virtues of female suffrage were meant to counter the anti-suffrage slant of many city newspapers.

Farmers-turned-publishers Ira and Emma Pack saw the need for such a journal in Topeka, Kansas, in 1890. They founded the *Farmer's Wife*, an eight-page tabloid aligning itself with the Farmer's Alliance, an organization that unionized farmers to fight oppression. (At that time, the Alliance was one hundred thousand strong in Kansas alone.) On the surface, the *Farmer's Wife* seemed devoted to the broad cause of improving life for rural women. But, for the Packs, that cause had a lot to do with giving women the right to vote.

The inaugural issue in July 1891 featured a piece by Bina A. Otis, the wife of congressman John Otis, on aligning women's rights with farmers' rights.

> *We are on the eve of a revolution equal to that of our forefathers when they rebelled against the tyranny of the mother country. They fought for the land of the free and the home of the brave, and are we going to permit the same country to become the land of the rich and the home of the slave, and will we leave as a legacy to our*

*children a country so covered with mortgages, bonds
and other forms of debt, that all through their lives
they will feel that they have a mill-stone around their
necks? I say no. Thank God the awakening has come.
The Alliance is to be our leader and will take us safely
into the promised land, where the farmers shall have
their just dues. This great reform movement is before
us. It is for the protection of our homes; and who can
be more interested in the homes of the country than the
American women?*

The paper became increasingly focused on rallying women across the state and country, and in the fourth issue, October 1891, editor Emma announced the creation of the National Women's Alliance. She declared her journal to be its "official organ."

Emma led the organization with another Kansan, Fannie McCormick, and eventually was joined by vice presidents in twenty-six states.

Emma wrote the following year, "No man is worthy the name of husband who will not do all in his power to place in woman's hand that great weapon, the ballot, that she may be able to help suppress these terrible wrongs and no American woman who is not dead to all the God given motherly instincts within her will quietly sit with folded hands and say they have all the rights they need."

The rhetoric became increasingly aggressive, and the *Farmer's Wife* gained national prominence. Circulation numbers are unknown, but the paper was among the most influential of its kind.

"Now, be men worthy of the name, and all, black and white alike, put your shoulder to the wheel and let the stars and stripes wave over free women as well as free men. Will you?" asked an article in the September 1893 issue. "If so, let every man who is in favor of the amendment carrying, send us $1.00 and the names of two people, men or women, who are not in favor of suffrage, and we will send *The Farmer's Wife* and convert them. We know we can with the host of contributors we have on the suffrage question. We believe there is no person who will read our paper who can help becoming converted."

The paper was sure to maintain regular sections on fashion, recipes, child-rearing, and agricultural news, but the *Farmer's Wife* had become a voice for the advancement of women. Each issue also featured about a page of news regarding the Populist Party, taking care to highlight the role Kansas women had played.

In November 1892, the *Farmer's Wife* reported that the Populists and Republicans in the Kansas legislature would present the option of equal suffrage to voters for the second time, during the November 1894 general election. In the lead-up to this vote, the *Farmer's Wife* and its suffragist agenda reached a fever pitch. Heartened by neighboring Colorado becoming the first state to grant women's suffrage in 1893, the national movement again focused its energies on Kansas. More than three thousand people attended a May 1894 suffragist meeting in Topeka, which included speeches by Pack, Otis, Anthony, and fellow activists Annie Diggs and Annie Shaw. Blue flags were waved at such gatherings, showing a star for each state with full suffrage for women (now with Colorado and Wyoming making up the very small constellation).

Meanwhile the *Farmer's Wife* went about endorsing pro-women candidates and even suggesting that elected officials should fear for their political future if they did not support women's right to vote. The message became clearer and clearer with epigrams such as this:

Give our women encouragement and victory is yours.

Be as true to the women as they are to you.

Don't give us taffy; we are too old for that.

Give the women a suffrage plank: you may have the rest.

*Rule the women out and the reform movement
is a dead letter.*

Put 1000 women lecturers in the field and reform is here.

The paper also endeavored to arm its readers with talking points and counter-arguments regarding women's right to vote. The May 1894 issue ran the transcript of a speech by Annie Diggs, who pointed out the weak arguments against suffrage.

"It is said that the women can't vote and go to the polls without neglecting their babies and household duties. I notice that we can go to church, or the theater, or a circus, or into society without anybody, not even the editors, howling about the neglected babies. It doesn't take near as long to go to the polls, but the moment we go there the men for the first time in their lives begin to worry about the little ones. It is said that we can't go to the polls in safety. I have gone a great many times and I would rather go there than to the post-office on a crowded day."

Following years of toil and organizing among suffragists from Kansas and beyond, as well as a groundswell of pro-suffrage rhetoric from influential papers such as the *Farmer's Wife*, Kansas citizens voted down the proposed amendment.

After twenty-eight issues, from July 1891 to October 1894, the *Farmer's Wife* folded.

Just as the suffragists' loss at the 1859 Wyandotte Constitutional Convention couldn't put out the flame lit by Clarina Nichols, the loss at the polls in 1894 couldn't put out the wild prairie fire that the *Farmer's Wife* had fanned. Kansas women—including rural women—continued to fight for the vote, often abandoning party lines to instead align themselves with a single objective. In just under two decades all the state's major political parties had gotten on board with women's suffrage. On November 5, 1912, the third time was a charm—nearly a decade before the Nineteenth Amendment to the U.S. Constitution, Kansas became the eighth state to give women full voting rights.

THE FATHER OF BASKETBALL

1898

If you know basketball, you know the University of Kansas Jayhawks.

KU has one of the most storied college basketball programs in the country, with frequent trips through the NCAA Tournament bracket and national championships in 1952, 1988, and 2008. Some of the greatest college coaches in history spent time there, from Phog Allen to Roy Williams, and NBA legends like Wilt Chamberlain and Danny Manning got their start on the floor of Allen Fieldhouse. And that floor they played on, James Naismith Court, is named after the man who started it all.

In 1890, young James Naismith scrapped his plan to devote his life to the Christian ministry and instead left his native Canada to serve as director of physical education at a YMCA in Springfield, Massachusetts. The next year, he was charged with creating a game that would keep students active throughout the winter months between football and lacrosse. Aiming to avoid off-season injuries for the players, Naismith wanted a game without the tough hits of football or the thronged players of soccer. So he hung a peach basket ten feet from the floor at each end of the gym, divided his class of eighteen young men into two teams, and sent them onto the floor with thirteen rules. Thus, basketball was born in December 1891.

After receiving his medical degree in 1898, Naismith moved to Kansas, where he would live for the next forty-one years.

Naismith served as KU's first physical education instructor, a role in which he demanded of students not only athletic development but moral and spiritual self-reflection. "With him, questions of physical development inevitably led to questions of moral development, and vice versa," one of his students said. Naismith conducted physical exams and kept medical records for male undergraduates, ultimately helping establish a student health service.

Naturally, Naismith also became the university's first basketball coach. He coached the track team, as well. But he wasn't thrilled with those roles. Ironically, he didn't take sports terribly seriously. His philosophy on athletics bore little resemblance to the rabid devotion of today's sports fans and players. He believed that games, even the one of his own invention, should be played for fun and for health, not for high-stakes competition.

One of his grandsons and namesakes, Jim Naismith, recalled the attitude of his "Papa Jimmy" for the *New York Times* in a 1991 interview marking the centennial anniversary of the sport.

"I was a terrible basketball player," the younger Naismith recalled. "I couldn't dribble, I couldn't pass and I certainly couldn't hit the basket. Not that my grandfather would have cared. To him, other things in life were always more important."

James Naismith's lackluster interest in winning showed. Over the course of nine seasons, from 1898 to 1907, he coached only two winning seasons. Today, James Naismith—the father of basketball—remains the only basketball coach in University of Kansas history to have ended his career with a losing record (55–60).

Naismith continued serving as a professor of physical education on the KU faculty and went on to write two books: *The Basis of Clean Living* in 1919 and *Basketball: Its Origin and Development,* published in 1941 after his death. Realizing a childhood dream, he was ordained as a Presbyterian minister in 1916 and led services at the KU chapel, the local YMCA, and for the First Kansas Regiment stationed near Mexico during World War I. He also traveled to France during the war, bringing sports and their therapeutic effects to army bases.

Naismith might have turned away from basketball, but he helped shape it during those few coaching years at KU. He tweaked the rules—like when he added the act of dribbling the ball to the rule book in 1900—and groomed one of the finest basketball coaches in history, Forrest "Phog" Allen. Allen lettered three years on Naismith's team and ultimately took the coaching reins himself when Naismith retired from the post in 1907. He would coach forty-nine seasons, all but ten of those at KU, finishing his career with an astounding 771–233 record. He earned the nickname "Phog" for his "foghorn" voice booming from the bench; today, "Beware the Phog" is among Jayhawks fans' most beloved aphorisms.

Allen's important contributions to the sport included lobbying to instate basketball as an Olympic sport in 1936; recruiting Wilt Chamberlain to the University of Kansas team; leading the United States team to a gold medal in the 1952 Summer Olympics in Finland; and creating the National Association of Basketball Coaches, which later founded the NCAA Tournament. And, where his mentor, James Naismith, is known as the "Father of Basketball," Allen became known as the "Father of Basketball Coaching"—he helped mold numerous Hall of Fame coaches, including Dean Smith, Adolph Rupp, Dutch Lonborg, and Ralph Miller.

As the game of basketball continued to evolve, Naismith didn't always approve; the elimination of the center jump—where each team once jumped for the ball after each score—in his opinion too greatly disadvantaged the team who had just scored. He did successfully campaign for revisions to his liking: the three-point shot from beyond a drawn line, and the all-important shot clock, which forces the offensive team to shoot the ball within a number of seconds. "Scoring is important, but not all-consuming," Naismith told the *Saturday Evening Post*. "I think speed is. Speed, passing, and the unexpected."

Phog Allen persuaded Naismith to travel from Kansas to Berlin as a guest of honor at the first Olympic basketball game. At the suggestion of the National Association of Basketball Coaches, colleges and universities across the country raised money for Naismith's trip by charging an extra penny for admission to games during the 1935–36 season.

Grandson Jim got to tag along with Naismith in 1936 when he tossed up the first ball for the Olympic Trials at Madison Square Garden in New York City. Naismith, age seventy-four and en route to Berlin, was grumpy about something.

"He was happy basketball was going to be played in the Olympics that August, but he was disappointed that it wasn't serving the purpose it was meant to: a game you played for sportsmanship and to use the winter months," Jim Naismith remembered.

Nonetheless, Dr. Naismith called the Olympic game—in which the United States beat Canada, 19–8, outdoors in the rain—the happiest moment of his life. He returned to America convinced that basketball would thrive abroad but with doubts about the game's future in his own country.

He couldn't have been more wrong.

By the start of World War II, a basketball team could be found at just about every school in America. In 1939, the year that Naismith died, the National Collegiate Athletic Association started its postseason tournament, now one of the most religiously watched sporting events in the world. And, while the sport is played at the professional level in more than one hundred countries, basketball remains a quintessentially American game. It's also the only major sport today truly invented by an individual person, rather than finding its roots in a much older sport (football stems from rugby, baseball from a game called "rounders," and so on). Gone are the peach baskets, but Naismith's game remains strikingly true to his 1891 vision. The billions of dollars that go into the sport at the college and professional levels, though, are another matter with which Dr. Naismith might have taken issue. He himself turned down a great deal of money to be a cigarette spokesman—an unthinkable endorsement for such a clean-living proponent.

"He never thought of making money out of basketball," Jim Naismith told the *Times*. "If he had, he would have patented it. He wasn't interested in money."

The Father of Basketball is honored at the Naismith Memorial Basketball Hall of Fame in Springfield, Massachusetts, where he invented the game, and he is buried in Lawrence, Kansas, where he watched it develop into a force on the world athletic stage. The University of Kansas road in front of Allen Fieldhouse, the famed basketball arena named for his pupil Phog Allen, bears the name Naismith Drive.

HATCHET JOB

1899–1901

Nearly six feet tall, Carry Nation was a large woman with an even larger mission at the turn of the last century—to mop up every last drop of booze in the country.

In 1899, Nation put on her best bonnet and stormed into Mort Strong's saloon. She cursed the owner and the bar's inhabitants, decrying the evils of alcohol. Prohibition had been the law in Kansas for a decade, but liquor was easy to come by in most communities. This, Nation believed, violated not only the law but the teachings of the Bible.

The saloon owner promptly hauled Nation back out the front door and, crying, Nation began to sing before the crowd of hundreds that had gathered to witness the spectacle. Fellow members of the Medicine Lodge Women's Christian Temperance Union, including the wife of the town's Baptist minister Wesley Cain, joined in the song. The rest of the crowd either hurled insults or joined the anti-drinking uprising.

Nation would return to cause a similar ruckus several more times, finally succeeding in convincing city officials to close down the illegal operation. Nation and her fellow female crusaders were overjoyed. They had tasted victory. But Nation wasn't done. Mort Strong's saloon had been but one of seven establishments selling alcohol in Medicine Lodge. As far as Nation was concerned, it was one down, six to go.

Born in Kentucky in November 1846, Nation developed her deep Christian faith during years of studying the Bible as a sickly, bedridden youth. In her early twenties, she married physician Charles Gloyd in Belton, Missouri. Unfortunately, Gloyd turned out to be a pitiful alcoholic who eventually drank himself to death, leaving Nation alone with a baby daughter. It was this experience that led to her extreme views on alcohol.

She supported herself, her daughter, and her mother-in-law for several years as a teacher in Warrensburg, Missouri, but ultimately lost her job. Soon she married Christian minister David Nation, who was a much better fit with Nation's moral standards—a professional man of God, a Union veteran of the Civil War, a lawyer, editor of the *Warrensburg Journal* and with no alcohol problem to boot. But they fought tirelessly; Carry often wrote his sermons—peppering them with assaults on liquor and tobacco—and attempted to take over at the pulpit, while David did not share her zeal for teetotaling.

In 1890, the couple moved to Texas and then to Kansas, where David would serve as pastor in the small town of Holton. Nation was thrilled to move to a Prohibitionist state, assuming she would find a land full of fellow loathers of liquor. She was wrong, of course.

Nation's continued intervention in her husband's ministry led him to resign, but she continued to make use of him as a successful lawyer prosecuting liquor offenses in Medicine Lodge. Meanwhile, she helped found a local chapter of the Women's Christian Temperance Union, which advertised slogans such as, "Lips that touch liquor shall not touch ours." As the organization's "jail evangelist," she counseled drunks in the local jail on the sordid nature of whiskey. But her real infamy came from saloon-busting.

After successfully shutting down Mort Strong's saloon, Nation set her sights on the drinking establishment of Henry Durst. Here, her dramatic display involved kneeling and praying at the front door. Having lured Durst outside his saloon, Nation sprang to her feet, grabbed him by the coat, and warned that he would burn in hell if he didn't close up shop. She promised to onlookers that she would lead prayer groups outside Durst's door twice a day until Durst came to the Lord, or until disaster befell his saloon. Durst responded by closing and leaving town.

Four more clandestine bars soon closed in the wake of Nation's anti-alcohol blitz. Six down, one to go.

The last of Nation's targets in Medicine Lodge was not a bar but rather a druggist known for supplying locals with alcohol. In February 1900, when she and Temperance Union sisters caught wind of his receiving a keg delivery, they headed to the drugstore. Nation rolled the keg into the street and, wielding a sledgehammer, smashed into it. As the alcoholic contents streamed into the gutter, she lit it on fire. Despite a local doctor rallying to the druggist's defense in a subsequent trial—he insisted he had given a permit to sell a particular brandy—the town's last alcohol vendor packed up and left.

Wild with success, Nation felt inspired to take her crusade outside her own town. Many of the jailbirds she ministered had confessed to finding their liquor supply in nearby Kiowa. So, in June 1900, she abandoned her prayer tactics and readied for brute force. With stones, bottles, and a billiard ball, she pummeled Kiowa's three saloons. Local law enforcement wasn't sure what to do—Nation had destroyed business operations, but illegal ones. She dared the police to arrest her. They didn't.

Six months later, Nation would target Wichita, the state's ultimate prize for anti-alcohol activists. The largest city in Kansas, Wichita was a distribution hub through which much of the state's illegal alcohol flowed. Growing ever bolder, this time Nation traded stones for a heavy iron rod.

The Hotel Carey on Wichita's hoppin' Douglas Avenue boasted a lavish saloon with an ornate mirror behind the long bar, a large nude painting of Cleopatra (*Cleopatra at the Bath,* by Wichita artist John Noble), and plenty of drinkers. Just after Christmas in 1900, Nation would show the place an even rowdier time than it was used to.

She bellowed threats of hellfire to the bartender and patrons; she pummeled the nude painting, which she found as offensive as bourbon; with her iron rod, she cleared the shelves and bar of bottles and glasses, creating an impressive symphony of shatter and splash. This time, she was taken in by police, shouting as she went, "You have put me in here a cub, but I will come out roaring like a lion, and I will make all hell howl." The prosecutor later dropped the charges based on his doubts about the soundness of Nation's mental state.

Nation had used prayer, insults, threats, stones, pool balls and bludgeons to administer the gospel of temperance. In January 1901, though, she adopted a real weapon—a sharp, heavy hatchet.

She would put it to use in Topeka first, one cold and early morning. Gruffly turned away by men guarding the doors of the first barroom—whose owner had been warned of Nation's intentions—Nation and two other women crossed snowy Kansas Avenue to bust into the elegant Senate Bar. Together, they splintered the bar, chairs, and cigar cases, and obliterated the bottles and glassware. "Smash, women, smash!" was Nation's battle cry. The only man in the place failed to run them out by firing two shots into the ceiling. Finally, the women were arrested, though the Women's Christian Temperance Union promptly posted their bail.

Nation's fame swelled. She received letters from across Kansas and beyond, asking her to bust up the saloons of this and that town. She took her hatchet to Iowa, Chicago, St. Louis, Kansas City, Cincinnati, New York, California, even England and Canada. As she traveled, she stopped to give fiery lectures to crowds of hundreds. She distributed a national newsletter, the *Smasher's Mail*. She sold tiny souvenir hatchets to pay the fines for her many arrests.

Nation was a national celebrity, but not everyone was a fan. One prominent Wichitan wrote that "Mrs. Nation's use of the hatchet in breaking into buildings, destroying furniture and disturbing the peace . . . should be treated by the courts precisely as the law requires them to treat other burglars. . . . Kansas is just now suffering deeply in the estimation of all substantial men in the East whom I meet. Remarks I am obliged to hear about the 'instability of society there,' 'lawlessness of professed good men,' 'low grade of civilization,' etc. are not easy to bear and are hard to refute."

Nation's own husband disdained her tactics for a more personal reason—she was never home. He was granted a divorce on grounds of desertion, sealing the irony that many historians have noted: Nation's first marriage was destroyed by a love of alcohol (her husband's), and her second marriage was destroyed by a hatred of alcohol (her own). She didn't appear to miss David, of course, and once said that "Men are nicotine-soaked, beer-besmirched, whiskey-greased, red-eyed devils."

Nation carried on with her travels and raids nearly until her death in 1911. Her legacy would be stories of destruction, not lasting change for the American people; Prohibition lost its hold in the 1930s, and Nation's daughter died in an insane asylum as an alcoholic.

FIRST FLIGHT

1904

The girl wanted to build a roller coaster.

She had traveled with her family from their comfortable home in Atchison, Kansas, to the 1904 St. Louis World's Fair. There, wonders abounded: a palace lit up with electricity, a Filipino village, x-ray machines, typewriters, primitive versions of the airplane. But what enchanted the girl was the roller coaster.

Just seven years old, she wasn't allowed to ride the roller coaster, but she returned home determined to create a similar experience. Amelia, her sister, and a neighbor kid set about constructing their own roller coaster atop a small shed. The finished product involved planks of wood—greased to slickness with lard—and a wooden crate to sit in. After the first and last unsuccessful ride down the "tracks," Amelia proclaimed it to be "just like flying."

Flying would be the theme of the young girl's life. Born in summer 1897 in Atchison, Amelia Mary Earhart was an adventurous child there on the banks of the Missouri River. She and her sister, Muriel, wore bloomers—baggy pants, of sorts—rather than dresses during playtime, and they preferred barreling down snow-covered hills on boys' sleds to dolls and dress-up. Their mother, Amy, let them play however they wished, despite the rigid gender roles of the times. Their parents called them "Meely" and "Pidge"—much less feminine names than Amelia and Muriel. The girls asked their father for BB guns, rifles, and footballs as holiday gifts, and he happily obliged.

About a year after the failed roller coaster project, Amelia's father, Edwin, closed his floundering Atchison law office in favor of a position with the Rock Island Railroad in Des Moines, Iowa. He and Amy left Amelia and Muriel with their affluent grandparents in Atchison while they traveled north to settle into a new home. The girls ended up staying there for two years.

The lovely, riverside home of Judge Alfred and Amelia Otis faced the wide, breathtaking Missouri River, on whose hilly, tree-lined banks famed explorers Lewis and Clark once camped. The white, two-story home was built at the beginning of the Civil War and featured the ornate touches of the Victorian period: welcoming porches, etched-glass windows, high ceilings, grand doorways, expensive wallpaper, and rich wood trim.

Amelia knew the place well, as her family had spent many holidays there. She knew the butler's pantry, where she and her sister sometimes ate lunch; the formal dining room, where she joined her grandparents for dinners cooked by servants; the second parlor, full of books that delighted her; the upstairs bedroom with the spool bed in which she was born; the smaller room across the hall, where she stayed, and its screened window providing an unbroken view of the river she loved.

It was a familiar place, full of love, but for Amelia and Muriel, life in the grand home was much more prim and proper than it had been under their parents' care. Grandfather Alfred was an eminent citizen of Atchison—a retired U.S. District Court judge, president of the Atchison Savings Bank, and chief warden of Trinity Episcopal Church. And Grandmother Amelia was a traditional woman of her time, frowning on her namesake granddaughter's proclivity for wearing pants and digging in the muddy Missouri River banks. Under her roof, Amelia and Muriel would wear lace on their dresses and curls in their hair.

Amelia did her best to resist her grandmother's plan to mold a proper young lady. When she was supposed to be practicing her manners, she was designing a trap to catch stray chickens. When she was supposed to be sitting with knitting needles, she was outside running with a football.

When Amelia was nine, her father gave her a .22-caliber Hamilton rifle for Christmas. Amelia, having read that rats were spreading the bubonic plague near the Panama Canal, thought she would do her grandparents the service of killing every rat in their barn. When a rat she had shot managed to get away, Amelia honored the hunting rule that no wounded animal should be left to suffer. She waited and waited outside the rat's hole until, finally, it emerged and received its death blow from Amelia's gun. Amelia was late for dinner, and her grandmother was horrified. The gun was taken away.

But Amelia and her sister managed to turn even harmless childhood games into dirty, sweaty exercise. With two of their Atchison cousins, the girls created a game called "Bogie," in which they rode an old, abandoned carriage into imaginary worlds and evaded monsters and attackers among hay bales and outbuildings. By the time they returned to the house, they would be covered in dust and cobwebs, their voices hoarse from screaming.

On snowy days, Amelia joined other Atchison children in sledding down the town's abundant hills. But, instead of sitting in a mannerly posture, as girls were taught to do, Amelia would lie down against her sled and fling herself down the slope alongside the boys (a tactic she later would claim saved her life, as she once accidentally zoomed under a horse).

Sharpshooting, monster-busting, and sledding weren't so easy in the skirts Grandmother Amelia insisted upon. The young Amelia later would write in her autobiography that, along with discriminatory social customs and lack of training, impractical clothing kept girls from succeeding in sports and other physical endeavors typically reserved for men.

In 1908, Amelia and Muriel finally joined their parents in Iowa, but Kansas would remain close to Amelia's heart. The boldness she honed under her grandmother's disapproving eye was the same boldness with which she would tackle her life's pursuit—aviation—under society's disapproving eye.

Once she left home, Amelia had a brief stint at a school near Philadelphia and then treated wounded World War I soldiers at a military hospital in Toronto. She went back to school, this time as a premedical student at Columbia University in New York, but eventually followed her parents to their new home in California. It was there that Amelia discovered flying. She took lessons and even managed to buy her own airplane. Flying thrilled her like nothing else could.

So, when Amelia later worked as a social worker in Boston, Massachusetts, she was still dreaming of the pilot's life and pondering what it meant to be a woman in her twenties craving a profession reserved for men. She had a brief engagement to a New England man but called it off—her heart wasn't in it. Her heart was in aviation, and she feared that marriage and its trappings would keep her earthbound (though she would later marry a man who supported and promoted her aspirations). Not long after breaking her engagement, she wrote a poem about the meaning of courage, seeming to resolve on paper that she would follow her passion, regardless of society's ideas about women. She would not deny her desire to be a pilot.

She seized on that desire, and in short time, she was piling up accolades: the first woman pilot to cross the Atlantic Ocean; the first woman to receive the presidential honor of the Distinguished Flying Cross; the first president of the Ninety-Nines organization of women pilots; the first woman to fly nonstop, coast to coast; and the first person to fly solo over the Pacific Ocean. By the time she was thirty years old, Earhart was a bona fide celebrity.

But she never forgot Kansas. She made time on cross-country flights to stop by her old stomping grounds. "I love the middle west," she told a reporter on the East Coast. "When the nose of my plane or my car, is turned westward, I have a feeling of pleasurable excitement."

In 1928, the same year Earhart became the first woman to fly solo, round-trip, across the United States, she visited Atchison and then greeted cheering school children in York, Nebraska. In 1933, by then known as the "First Lady of the Air," Earhart lectured on flying to more than a thousand people in Emporia, Kansas, stopping next in Leavenworth, Atchison, Kansas City, and Lawrence. She loved her home state and meant to spread the word of aviation there.

In June 1935, Earhart returned to Atchison to help the Kansas governor Alfred M. Landon kick off a weekend convention. She rode on a flower-filled float in a mile-long military parade through the streets of her hometown before speaking to thirty-five hundred fans at Memorial Hall, where she recalled her deceased grandparents' home and the sledding thrills of her childhood.

Just two years later, Earhart would attempt her most ambitious aviation feat yet—a twenty-nine-thousand-mile flight around the equator. She and crew member Fred Noonan flew out of Miami, Florida, on June 1, 1937, and successfully journeyed twenty-two thousand miles to New Guinea by month's end. On July 2, they left

New Guinea for a remote island in the middle of the Pacific Ocean. Their plane disappeared; Earhart and her friend would never be seen again. The cause of their disappearance, of course, remains unknown and is one of the great mysteries of the twentieth century.

Earhart can still be spotted, however, all over Atchison, Kansas, in the form of sculptures, museum exhibits, and a one-acre landscape mural in her image. And nearby is the International Forest of Friendship, planted by Earhart's old Ninety-Nines organization of women pilots. The forest, a memorial and celebration of aviation and aerospace pioneers, includes trees representing fifty states and thirty-five countries; among them stands a bronze, life-size statue of Amelia Earhart.

EISENHOWER'S ROOTS

1909

The 1909 yearbook of Abilene High School, *Helianthus,* contained a creative little feature wherein a member of the class wrote as though from the future, describing what had become of the graduating seniors. In the yearbook section, "Class Prophecy," young Cecilia Curry mentioned a handful of graduating seniors, but two brothers named Edgar and Dwight Eisenhower were the focus. And, among the two, Edgar was the real star.

> *"Oh, I will have to call Bess and show this to her."*
> *Here she is now waiting for me. "Look here, Bess, what*
> *do you think of this. I can fancy I see Harry leading*
> *the parade, on a beautiful white charger and feeling,*
> *I expect, like George Washington did when he was*
> *breaking the young colt, which his mother prized so*
> *highly."*

*The politics always interested me a little so I
thought I would run these over and all of a sudden I
recognized the name, Eisenhower. "If Eisenhower is
elected president this year it will make his third term."
Then I sat wondering if Edgar really would take the
chair the third time.*

*"Say Bess, do you know what has become of
Dwight?"*

*"Why yes! I hear about all the great men of the
world. He is professor of history in Yale. Speaking of
Yale reminds me that Bruce Hurd went there and is
now one of the judges of the Supreme court. I think our
class is surely a credit to dear old A.H.S., don't you?"*

Cecilia was almost right. It would be Dwight, of course, who
would go on to be a five-star general of the U.S. Army during World
War II and the popular thirty-fourth president of the United States.

But, growing up in small-town Kansas, it was indeed the elder
brother, Edgar, who attracted more attention. Edgar was the star
football player; Dwight played and loved sports but had a mind more
accurate than his arm, particularly in math and history studies.

Dwight Eisenhower was an average student, in terms of marks
in the classroom, but he had an incredible memory for names, dates,
and other data. Thus, he most enjoyed topics that had clear, right-or-
wrong answers, such as mathematics, with its definitive formulas and
equations. But his love was history. He voraciously consumed books
on world leaders, wars, and historical events, to such an extent that
his mother used withholding of history books as a punishment if he

skimped on chores or got into mischief. In high school, he aced the subject, prompting his teacher to give him lengthier, more sophisticated assignments than his fellow students received.

But Abilene High was hardly a sophisticated place of learning. When Eisenhower began there as a freshman in 1904, the school was situated on the first floor of City Hall, along with the fire bell and other public essentials. If firemen rang the bell, students sprang from their seats to serve as fire department volunteers. The town had just constructed a sewer system a year prior, and its streets remained unpaved (as they would until 1910). Abilene would construct a proper high school in 1905, but even that was a far cry from the New England prep school experience known to so many U.S. presidents.

Social class was a defining aspect of Eisenhower's formative years in Kansas, perhaps because lines were drawn so sharply between rich and poor in Abilene. The town was famous for its days as a cow town on the Chisholm Trail in the late 1800s, and kids like Eisenhower played their share of "Wild West" games, pretending to be Wild Bill Hickok or other gun-toting figures from the town's history. But by the time Eisenhower was growing up, survival in Abilene depended on money, not sharpshooting.

The Union Pacific and Santa Fe railroad tracks split Abilene into two parts: north and south. On the north side, houses were big and sturdy, fathers wore suits to work, and well-dressed children played in lovely lawns. On the south side, houses were modest, fathers came home covered in dirt or oil, and barefoot children wore hand-me-downs. That's where Eisenhower's childhood was spent.

He was actually born in Denison, Texas, where his father, David, took the family after a bad business deal in Abilene. David, a shopkeeper, had invested his entire inheritance in a partnership that went bust. Forced to follow work wherever it took him, he and his small family made their way south. It was a brief stay, though; after two years in Texas, David, wife Ida, and their three sons moved to Abilene in the spring of 1891.

They stayed for a short time on Southeast Sixth Street, just south of the railroad tracks, in a house with a steep roof and a tiny yard. David's small earnings at the Belle Springs Creamery couldn't afford more than that. But, when David's brother Abraham sold his dentistry practice and moved west, the family had an opportunity to live more comfortably. Abraham allowed David to rent the place, two blocks over on Southeast Fourth Street, with the option to buy it at a later date. The Eisenhowers moved once again.

The two-story, white frame house sat on an abundant, three-acre corner lot on the southern edge of town. Because the house sat close to the street, the backyard was all the bigger—perfect for a household full of growing boys. And the rest of the ample land, with its big barn—complete with horse stalls and a large hay loft—was perfect for raising animals and produce. The family tended a half-acre garden of tomatoes, potatoes, onions, beans, peas, cabbage, radishes, lettuce, corn, and strawberries. They also planted hay and field corn to feed their livestock, which included two cows, for milk and meat, along with chickens for eggs and meat. They also raised ducks, guinea hens, pigs, and rabbits. The Eisenhowers even cured their own meat in a smokehouse on the property.

The operation was rounded out by a small orchard of fruit trees—cherry, apple, pear—and a tiny grape vineyard.

It was a beautiful, self-sustaining way of life, but it required a lot of work. Dwight and Edgar planted and tended the vegetable garden, built the fire in the stove in the early morning hours, and much more. Their most dreaded duty, however, was selling vegetables.

The older boys had to load a buggy full of extra vegetables (the garden's bounty was far too great for one family), hitch it to a horse, and ride through town—namely the affluent north side—selling the produce. It was often humiliating work, with well-to-do households sometimes haggling the poorly dressed young brothers for lower prices on their lovingly grown tomatoes.

In grade school, these were the boys' closest encounters with "north siders." Their elementary school, Lincoln, was easily viewed from the Eisenhowers' front door and enrolled mostly "south siders."

Then, in seventh grade, Edgar and Dwight found themselves in the socioeconomic mix of Garfield Junior High, whose student body came from all over town. The boys wore their usual hand-me-downs to school, with Dwight even sporting his mother's old button-top shoes, making them the laughing stock of Garfield's north-side children. In this challenging climate, Dwight learned how to take a punch; a particularly legendary dust-up involved Dwight, short and skinny at the age of thirteen (by now known as "Little Ike" to Edgar's "Big Ike"), and a quick-footed kid named Wesley Merrifield. After a proper challenge had been leveled, the two met when school ended. Merrifield was by far the better boxer, landing a handful of painful punches for every smack that Dwight managed to deliver, but something was different about Merrifield's small opponent—he wouldn't fall down. Maybe it was because Dwight had grown up getting pummeled by his older brother, Edgar, and could take a hit. Maybe it was because his own wild temper (he once hurled a brick at his younger brother Arthur) wouldn't let him quit. But, punch after punch, a bloodied Dwight wouldn't back down. A group of children cheered the fighters on, but the fight seemingly would not end. An hour had passed, and Dwight was still standing. Arms continued swinging—mostly Merrifield's—and then two hours had passed. Merrifield finally gave up. He had given Dwight a solid beating, but the tough kid from the south side of the tracks had never hit the ground.

Physical fortitude became much more serious business when, in ninth grade, Dwight fell and cut his leg on the way home from school. The wound became infected and turned into a full-blown case of blood poisoning; Dwight's leg swelled up, streaks of red running along the discolored flesh. Amputation, the doctor said. Lose the leg or lose your life. But Dwight refused. For weeks, he fought the pain and the disorientation of his condition, and against all odds, he beat the infection and kept his leg.

It was this sort of pride that carried Eisenhower into Abilene High School. He wasn't about to let his humble roots cost him any opportunities, just as he hadn't let a case of blood poisoning cost him his leg. Sure, he wasn't accepted to the "Bums of Lawsy Lou," a pretentious student organization marked by social standing, but Eisenhower won friends nonetheless with his earnestness, revealed by a crooked smile and uncombed hair. Sure, he had little clout to impress girls, around whom he was extremely shy, but he won dates nonetheless with his blonde hair and sharp intellect, demonstrated at the political debates that would erupt at Tip Top Restaurant in town. There, Dwight showed an uncanny ability to deconstruct and dismantle a fellow man's argument.

Dwight also had a profound sense of justice on the football field, where his size made him an underdog. He would become outraged when an opponent or teammate "played dirty" or demonstrated any level of disrespect; once, his teammates refused to shake hands with an African-American opponent, but Dwight saw to it. When the entire team, north siders and all, lacked means to travel to a game in a neighboring town, Dwight led the group in a train-jumping exercise—they rode to the town for free, via freight train. But it was when the team lacked adequate equipment and uniforms that Dwight made his first stroke of true leadership, founding the Abilene High School Athletic Association. In his role as president of the group, Dwight led the players to pool their own money and do fundraising around town. It was a success, and the organization was validated with an appearance in the yearbook—the same one that imagined another Eisenhower, his brother, as president.

Dwight and Edgar graduated in 1909 with twenty other young men and women, but their initial paths were quite different. Dwight toiled full-time at the Belle Springs Creamery with his father, firing furnaces, making boxes, and washing cream cans. With his wages, he helped support his brother's first two years at the University of Michigan. But, before Dwight could take his own turn in college, another opportunity arose—enrollment in the United States Military Academy at West Point, New York. Dwight left Abilene in 1911, but he took with him the dignity and regard for social equality that he developed in his youth.

In 1947, while serving as chief of staff for the U.S. Army, Dwight reflected on his personal history that the small Kansas town of Abilene had "provided both a healthy outdoor existence and a need to work. These same conditions were responsible for the existence of a society which, more nearly than any other I have encountered, eliminated prejudices based upon wealth, race or creed, and maintained a standard of values that placed a premium upon integrity, decency, and consideration for others. Any youngster who has the opportunity to spend his early youth in an enlightened rural area has been favored by fortune."

Six years later, Eisenhower would be president of the United States.

THE GOAT-GLAND DOCTOR

1917

The Brinkley-Jones Hospital and Training School for Nurses kept goats.

Sure, the private hospital in a tiny town at the edge of the Flint Hills had normal medical fare, such as an X-ray machine, rows of scalpels, and operating tables. But the key to its signature treatment was the goats, who lived in a pen behind the large hospital building. People traveled from across the country to receive the goats' healing powers, administered by the diamond-ring-wearing, fast-talking, questionably trained Dr. John R. Brinkley.

Brinkley came to Milford, Kansas, in 1917 to set up shop as the town doctor. He had studied medicine for three years at Bennett College in St. Louis but, unable to pay the school, ultimately obtained a bogus degree at a Kansas City, Missouri, school called Eclectic Medical University. The place had a bad habit of awarding medical certificates to anyone who would pay for them. Because the school wasn't recognized by most states, he artfully obtained his medical license in Arkansas and then acquired a Kansas license for $25 by way of reciprocity, wherein one state recognizes the professional certifica-tions of another. It was a roundabout road, but Brinkley was ready to make good money in Milford, a remote town in which he could charge a sizable fee for long-distance house calls to rural areas.

Brinkley's life before Milford had been as unorthodox as his so-called education and licensure. Born in 1885 to a poor North Carolina doctor who had served as a medic for the Confederate Army, Brinkley had always dreamed of being a doctor. But just out of school in Kansas City, he found himself working at Swift Pack-ing Company, becoming intimately familiar with the anatomy of slaughtered livestock.

One animal held particular interest for Brinkley: the goat. While working at Swift, he learned that goats were immune to human dis-ease and that they were among the healthiest animals on the planet. Cattle and pigs got sick regularly enough, but goats were predictably robust and virile. It was at the packing company that Brinkley began to formulate the theory that would make him a rich man.

For the next two years, Brinkley—along with his second wife, Minnie, whom he had married without divorcing his first wife, with whom he had two daughters—moved from town to town in Kansas, looking for steady work as a doctor. His ear, nose, and throat prac-tice only lasted a month in Hays, in western Kansas, as the locals distrusted his character. He drew a wealth of customers in Fulton after curing an old couple's constipation, and with this success he purchased a fancy car and joined the local Masons and Shriners. But Brinkley soon found himself stationed at Fort Bliss in El Paso, Texas, serving under the Medical Officers Reserve during World War I. (Brinkley would recall valiantly tending to the health of more than two thousand recruits for months on end, but army records say he served one month and five days, almost all of which he was lying in the Fort Bliss hospital for nervous exhaustion.)

Discharged from the military, Brinkley returned to Fulton to find that another doctor had swooped in and taken his business. It was time to move again. An ad attempting to attract a doctor to Milford caught his eye in the *Kansas City Star*; the ad listed a population of two thousand, though it was actually more like two hundred.

Minnie cried at the prospect of starting over there, a town with nothing more than a bank, two mills, a small mercantile, and one rural post office route. But Brinkley insisted that the town was rife with opportunity.

Brinkley was still in debt from his Fulton hijinks but, gradually, he worked his way out of it. The major influenza outbreak of 1917 allowed him to establish trust and rapport with locals over the course of many house calls, and he performed minor surgeries for swollen tonsils or burst appendixes. Soon, Brinkley had a couple thousand in the bank. He was able to rent an office building, complete with living quarters and a drugstore at which Minnie ran the soda fountain. Brinkley presented himself smartly, wearing light suits, sharp spectacles, and a well-trimmed, auburn goatee. He felt sure that he was going places, and he would be ready when opportunity knocked.

Soon, a local farmer stopped by to chat privately about a certain medical condition. He was, well, impotent. Could the doctor help?

Brinkley's blue eyes must have twinkled, as he had waited for this moment for years now. Finally, he could test some of the ideas he had developed back at Swift Packing Company in Kansas City: specifically, his idea that implantation of goat testicles into a human male would result in increased sexual performance.

The farmer agreed to undergo the procedure and even agreed to supply the goat.

First, Brinkley transplanted slices of goat testicles into the farmer's own testicles. Next, he blocked the vas deferens on that side and transplanted a blood vessel and nerve to the new testicle hybrid (for what Brinkley termed "more nerve energization"). The whole procedure took less than fifteen minutes and cost $150.

The farmer was happy with the results; he reported a change in the bedroom, and gossip spread about the doctor's unique service.

The next goat-gland recipient, William Stittsworth, didn't stop with his own procedure. He made sure his wife received a goat ovary, as well. The couple had faced difficulty conceiving a child, but a year later the two had a baby boy, nicknamed "Billy."

More and more people came to Brinkley, and soon dozens of locals were walking around with bits of goat glands in their bodies. There was a bit of a learning curve, as some of these early patients found they began to emit an unpleasant animal musk; the trick, Brinkley learned, was to avoid stinky Angora goats and use only three-week-old male and yearling female Toggenburg goats.

While curing impotence was a buzz-worthy claim itself, Brinkley soon expanded the scope of his goat-gland theory. After operating on a resident of an insane asylum, Brinkley claimed he could cure insanity. He also claimed his procedure could cure high blood pressure, epilepsy, diabetes, and, yes, even cancer.

Brinkley was ready to capitalize on momentum for the goat-gland procedure. He hired an advertising executive to consult with him on public relations. The ad man saw a gold mine in the idea and encouraged him to gather testimonials from patients, target rural households with mailed pamphlets, and take out ads in one hundred of the nation's top newspapers.

The advertising blitz paid off; the chancellor of the law school at the University of Chicago himself underwent a goat-gland transplant and, delighted, saw to it that his school award Brinkley an honorary doctor of science degree. This exposure resulted in an onslaught of new patients from near and far, generating income that would allow Brinkley to build the Brinkley-Jones Hospital and Training School for Nurses. The place opened in September 1918 and included a drugstore, post office, barber, restaurant, and—fittingly for a hospital making use of goat testicles—a butcher shop.

Brinkley was on his way to real success, and he needed the town of Milford to catch up with him. He led a mission to incorporate the town, establish a city government, and install electricity, running water and sewer lines. Some residents objected to the increased taxes, but the town went forward with the changes Brinkley proposed, soon paving main roads, building sidewalks, and establishing a high school.

The hospital drew a steady stream of patients, providing economic vigor to the town. Brinkley and his wife were local celebrities; they "gave back" to Milford by giving away turkeys during the holiday season, sponsoring a baseball team called the Brinkley Goats, and building a Methodist church (though the bishop wouldn't allow it to be called "John R. Brinkley Methodist Episcopal Church"). They even kept a live bear caged in their front yard for the enjoyment of children passing by—until, one night, it made noise incessantly, and Brinkley shot it to death.

Brinkley was getting a reputation for being a loose cannon. He appeared to have a drinking problem, carrying a gun in public or transforming into a mad man who chased patients with a knife if they didn't pay up. On at least one occasion, he was arrested for shooting up the town and found guilty of disturbing the peace.

Nonetheless, Brinkley's business grew. He had an offer to operate on former president Woodrow Wilson but refused to a condition of secrecy. One newspaper falsely reported that the entire country of Japan had embraced Brinkley's procedure. In 1922, a *Los Angeles Times* editor brought Brinkley to California, pressed the state medical board to grant the man a temporary permit, and then underwent the surgery himself; subsequently, Brinkley received rave reviews in the newspaper and went on to operate on aging movie stars in need of a sexual boost.

Brinkley detested the hot, humid Kansas summer and took to leaving town during that season; he would spread his work to Chicago, New York, and Connecticut. With his mounting income, the hospital received an addition, and Brinkley experimented with transplanting the testicles of deceased young humans, which were expensive and hard to come by. Then, he and Minnie—who had granted herself a nursing degree from her husband's hospital and was in charge of anesthetics—left the country altogether, taking goat-gland surgery all the way to Switzerland and the Far East: Shanghai, Saigon, and Singapore.

Patients continued to stream into Milford. By 1927, Brinkley had performed hundreds of operations and couldn't keep up with demand, though he was now charging $750. He was earning $1.5 million a year on his goat-gland scheme, not to mention another half million from prescriptions.

Along the way, Brinkley saw his share of backlashes. In 1921, when one happy patient celebrated Brinkley's method in a book, *The Goat Gland Transplantation,* the American Medical Association contacted the publisher with information on Brinkley's lackluster credentials, and the publication was halted. Connecticut, Brinkley's summertime stomping ground, revoked his license upon discovering his bogus degree. His application for a permanent medical license in California was denied, and Brinkley was charged with conspiracy to circumvent medical licensing requirements, though the charges were later dropped. He tried with little luck to take his practice to Europe; England wouldn't recognize his credentials, nor would Scotland or the University of Rome. He finally secured a degree at the University of Pavia in Italy, until they caught wind of his "eclectic" training and revoked it. His outrageous advertising got him expelled from the

American Medical Association, and a Chicago hospital sent him and his goats packing without an Illinois state license. In 1924, Henry Ford's newspaper called Brinkley a charlatan.

It would be wrong to suggest that Brinkley was the only one of his kind. Research into animal glands, organ and tissue, and their potential benefits to humankind was in vogue. Indeed, Brinkley's greatest professional nemesis, Dr. Max Thorek of Chicago, studied the transplantation of gorilla glands. But no one made a name for himself quite like Brinkley did.

This was largely due to his prowess in self-promotion. When Brinkley wasn't operating, he was giving lectures or ordering more advertising. And when radio became public media, Brinkley seized the opportunity, in 1923 establishing the fourth commercial station in the country and becoming the star of KFKB. His station featured programs covering health, country music, poetry, market news, the weather, and fundamentalist religious teachings. But it was all a cover for Brinkley's real objective. His nasaly voice, still with a tinge of North Carolina accent, spoke to the entire nation, mostly its rural factions, imploring them to seek his medical help. He thrilled men with the prospect of increased sexual virility, and delighted women by recognizing their sexual needs in a time when such matters weren't recognized, let alone discussed. "You owe it to yourself and your wife," he told men over the airwaves, just as he had written "Many and many wives come to me and say, 'Doctor, my husband is no good'" in one brochure.

The *Kansas City Star* described the craftiness of Brinkley's groundbreaking radio show:

> *In all the history of quackery there never was another system so perfectly and smoothly devised to rope in victims.*
> *. . . The system begins with his radio. From morning to*

night it operates, with orchestra music, old fiddlers, sing-
ers, and other entertainment. This . . . corresponds to
the banjo picker and singer of the street medical faker;
it attracts the public and holds it for the ballyhoo of the
faker himself and his lectures, the climax being the sale of
his fake remedies.

Brinkley's ballyhoo is in his radio lectures each day. In
these he describes the ailments of men, the symptoms of lost
manhood, and the sure remedy he has in his goat gland
operation. He invites correspondence through the mails;
that is the second step in his 'come-on' ballyhoo, and here is
the high spot of his system. Once a person writes to Brinkley
he is doomed from then on to receive a deluge of pamphlets,
testimonials, and urgings to go to Milford to be examined.

Responding to complaints by the American Medical Association, the Federal Radio Commission shut down KFKB in 1930. Brinkley sued on the grounds of censorship, but federal courts sided with the commission in a landmark decision. The same year, the Kansas Medical Board investigated forty-two deaths related to Brinkley's surgeries and revoked his license. The Goat-Gland Doctor's time in Kansas was running short.

He rallied by mounting a campaign for governor—a position from which he could transform the medical board to his liking. As a write-in candidate, he narrowly lost with 30 percent of the vote, and it's widely believed that state officials intervened in what was truly a win for Brinkley.

Brinkley moved his wife and small son south to Del Rio, Mexico, where he could continue his radio operation legally by blasting signals across the border into the United States. Thus, in the 1930s, despite the economic depression going on in the United States, Brinkley, his wife, and a young son lived in extravagance south of the border. Brinkley drove a custom-made Lincoln with gold-plated hub caps, or a sixteen-cylinder Cadillac with his name emblazoned on gold plate in thirteen places. He wore enormous diamond rings on his hands and kept a veritable zoo at his palatial new home—birds, giant tortoises, and penguins ill-suited for the hot climate. The animals moved about the fantastic grounds that featured a lily pond, spectacularly lit water fountains, and a huge pool with Brinkley's name in it.

But the coming decade would continue to unravel Brinkley's success. Ultimately, he was bankrupted by charges of medical malpractice, tax evasion, and mail fraud and died of heart failure in 1942.

COAL MINERS' DAUGHTERS

1921

It was Christmastime in southeast Kansas, but the wives and daughters of area coal miners were full of neither cheer nor good tidings—quite the opposite, in fact. They were mad as hell.

Their husbands, fathers, and brothers earned meager incomes for their families in the treacherous southeast Kansas coal mines, risking their lives wedging along dusty tunnels on their sides in order to put food on the table back home. They were lucky if they earned more than a dollar a day, and injury or death in the mines was common, with two hundred miners hurt or killed in 1921 in Crawford and Cherokee Counties alone. Thus, the period was marked by a number of workers' strikes, led by the Kansas Coal Miners' Union, in order to demand better wages and conditions for the men.

Labor strikes were extremely taxing on the miners' families, mostly immigrants from Germany, Slovenia, and even France and Italy, who had no financial reserves to fall back on in lieu of paychecks. But the families supported one another and were committed to getting their point across to the bigwigs at the coal companies. Short-term sacrifice was worth long-term gain, they told themselves. They would hold out until the workers got a fair shake, even if it meant shutting down coal excavation altogether.

So when the mining companies began hiring replacements for any men who went on strike, outrage reverberated through southeast Kansas. But a state law protected the big bosses; Kansas had made it illegal for union leaders to order strikes. This controversial move had received national attention the previous spring, when Samuel Gompers, president of the American Federation of Labor, debated Kansas governor Henry J. Allen in a packed Carnegie Hall in New York City. Gompers said any law preventing strikes was akin to slavery. Allen said it protected the interest of the public, who relied on industry production. Allen also insisted that Kansas men still possessed the "divine right to quit work," though no union leader should have the "divine right" to order a strike. The large crowd groaned and booed, and Gompers mocked Allen's point, stumping the governor with a question regarding what "divine right" existed to create laws governing all of the above. The crowd cheered.

Back in Kansas, Alexander Howat, head of the Kansas Coal Miners' Union, was in jail for his organizing shenanigans. He had refused to recognize or testify before the State Court of Industrial Relations in 1920, yelling from the balcony of his jail that it was "composed of three corporation lawyers appointed by that skunk of a Governor, Allen." A crowd of miners and their families had gathered to cheer his soliloquy, carrying American flags and banners reading "We are for the USA."

But, in 1921, replacements for striking workers marched into the mines. The new workers, most fraternity boys from area universities, were loathed by locals for rendering the strike moot; miners, their families, and other sympathizers called the temporary workers "scabs."

By the holiday season, the mothers, daughters, and sisters of the striking coal miners had had enough.

In mid-December, almost six thousand women—representing their husbands, fathers, and brothers in the 517 coal mines of southeast Kansas—gathered to protest the mining companies' use of replacement workers.

Together, they marched to the mine entrances carrying American flags and hungry babies. They themselves were hungry, and they looked the part in their tattered coats and threadbare skirts. But, enlivened by their mission, the women sang songs in their native tongues—German, Slovene, French, Italian—and raised an incredible ruckus wherever they went. They threw rocks at the "scabs," beat the mine bosses with brooms, and threatened the entire establishment that had forsaken their men and thus their homes and families. Other factions of the protest drove mile-long processions to mines, ordering workers to clear out or meet bodily harm.

Local police were utterly mystified as to how to proceed. Normally, a good clubbing would be in order, but these were women, with babies in tow.

Unencumbered by officials, the women succeeded in forcing workers to abandon their shifts. In some instances, when an operation knew the women were coming, they didn't even bother beginning work for the day. Newspapers reported forces of sheriffs and deputies standing idly, watching with slack jaws as the mob of women stormed various mines. The protesters grew bolder, firing pistols menacingly and setting off two explosions that debilitated a steam shovel in Crawford County.

Some of the protesters backed up their aggressive tactics with intellectual persuasion. One marcher, Fannie Wimler, wrote to the *Pittsburg Daily Headlight,* "What we want is our industrial freedom and liberty and we want our men to be good, true, loyal union men and 100 percent American citizens."

The point on citizenry was particularly relevant, as attitudes toward European immigrants were central to the issue. At the government level, there was talk of deporting un-nationalized troublemakers.

In the meantime, more immediate measures were required to stop the women from completely shutting down the coal mine production they'd successfully slowed. County officials asked for assistance from the state; soon, Governor Allen called in the National Guard. A command post, complete with an active machine gun company, was set up at the Stilwell Hotel in Pittsburg. Many locals believed the federal troops would be unnecessary if local officials would simply exert force rather than feebly stand by as the "weaker sex" stormed the mines. Others charged that deposed Kansas union leader Howat had masterminded the whole operation, though he claimed to be angry over the women's tactics and said he had nothing to do with it.

At the national level, the protesting women of southeast Kansas had ignited a national debate over not just unions' rights but women's roles in society. One headline read, "Amazons jeer guardsman." And a *New York Times* editorial charged that the women had exploited the very sexist ideologies to which they might normally object. "The plan seems to be effective for the present, but if perpetuated, how long will it be before the consideration which prevents the harsh treatment of these feminine mobs is abandoned? That consideration is based, really, on the assumption that women are the gentler sex, and therefore must be treated gently. But their claim to protection rests on their deserving as well as on their needing it, and if the desert ceases, the need will not be recognized forever."

Indeed, the "harsh treatment" avoided by local officials finally came into play. The National Guard, with its machine guns and menacing presence, curbed the protests, and county attorneys finally began issuing arrests for strike leaders, women or not.

As for the striking male workers, the press cast them as cowards who sent women to do their dirty work. One writer called them "too cunning to take the lead themselves in an aggressive fight to stop work in the mines." Another was shocked to witness a scene in which three National Guardsmen entered the town of Franklin to find women completely in charge. "They crowded close to the men while their husbands stood in the background," the reporter wrote. "There was some jeering of the soldiers by the women, but the husbands kept silent."

By the end of December, forty-nine women had been arrested and jailed, the union men had gone back to the mines, and many Americans had seen a version of womanhood they never imagined possible.

THE DIRTY THIRTIES

1935

The young farmer, Harvey Pickrel, could hardly believe his luck. He and his brother were passing through Great Bend, on the dry plains of central Kansas, chatting with a local farmer who had offered them an incredible deal. The man would sell them his "Go-Dig," a four-wheel crop cultivator, for next to nothing. The Go-Dig, mounted with sharp, metal disks and shovels, could cultivate four rows of earth at once as it was pulled across a field. It was a miraculous machine that would dramatically reduce the hours of backbreaking labor the two brothers spent on their father's farm to the north in Nebraska. In the throes of the Great Depression, they had weighed the financial sacrifice of purchasing such a machine. But now, it seemed, they could take it home for a dirt-cheap price.

"We don't use it anymore," the Kansas farmer said. "We can't raise corn. It's too dry."

So where was this bargain Go-Dig, Pickrel wondered.

The Kansas man pointed toward the barren, windswept field that once boasted glistening, green rows of cornstalks. Pickrel didn't see the cultivating machine.

"About all you can see is the top of it," the man said. "The rest is drifted under dirt."

Pickrel squinted his eyes. The land was a pitiful sight—heaps of brown dirt sloping against fences clogged with tumbleweeds. A long, severe drought had turned it to dust, and the powerful winds of the Great Plains had taken the topsoil with it, blowing the dirt through kitchen windows and whipping up terrifying, monstrous black dust clouds that turned the sky black. Pickrel had grown up helping his dad work the land, turning dirt with new plowing technologies, pushing for maximum crop output like everyone else did. That practice, coupled with months on end with little to no rain, had turned the land against them. Pickrel studied the Kansas man's field, finally making out bits of metal poking up from a large dirt drift. The Go-Dig was dirt cheap, all right. It could be theirs for a steal of a price—they just had to dig it out.

Kansas was at the heart of the Dust Bowl, and farmers struggled to survive. Wheat prices plummeted to twenty-five cents per bushel. Punishing, triple-digit temperatures seared the bone-dry landscape. Enormous swarms of grasshoppers ate whatever vegetation remained, even gnawing on the wooden handles of garden rakes, salty with gardeners' sweat. Each morning, women hung wet bed sheets over windows and doors, trying in vain to keep the thick dust from entering their homes, settling on dishes, tables, and everything else. At one point, geologists at the University of Wichita calculated that a five-million-ton cloud of dust, a mile thick, hung over their large city. Everyone prayed for rain.

On April 14, 1935, the ultimate dust storm rolled across the plains. The storm was called the Black Blizzard, and the day became known as Black Sunday. Complete darkness fell across the plains in the middle of the day, the sun so obstructed by dust that chickens went to roost, believing that nighttime had arrived. The wind blew seeds from the ground and moved automobiles thirty feet from where they had rested.

In Dodge City, eleven-year-old Louis Sanchez was used to the dust. For most of the years he could remember, he had been inhaling it, or watching it fall in muddy clumps from the wet sheets his mother hung about their humble dwelling in the Mexican part of town known as "the village." He had seen his young friends grow sick with lung problems from the omnipresent dust in the air, which exacerbated a tuberculosis outbreak within the village.

On April 14, donning his older brother's hand-me-down clothes, Sanchez went to the Dodge City public library to read the news of the day; the son of an immigrant railroad worker, Sanchez and his family didn't have a penny to spare to actually purchase a newspaper. Sanchez, having gotten his fill of news, left the library mid-afternoon and walked south toward KGNO, a radio station. Since his family didn't own a radio, Sanchez liked to hang out next to KGNO to listen to music. But, in the course of his walk from the library to the station—a distance of sixty feet or so—the air turned black.

An enormous dust cloud, worse than any Sanchez had seen, was rolling across Dodge City, blinding eyes and smothering mouths and noses. Sanchez had to get out of the storm, but he couldn't find the entrance to the radio station. His face stung as the racing wind blasted his face with sand. Finally, Sanchez found the door to KGNO and pulled it shut, the wind roaring behind him. Inside the building, the air was just as black. To reach the second-floor radio studio and whatever adults might be there, he crawled up the stairs on his hands and knees, unable to see.

Sanchez sat upstairs in the darkness. After half an hour, more people sought refuge there. They had been on their way to see a movie when the storm struck; they left their cars behind and felt their way along the pavement curb, darkened with dust by the time they reached shelter at the radio station.

The hours passed, with the black wind whipping outside the windows. Sanchez knew his mother would be worried about him and longed to run home, but it would be three hours before he could emerge from the KGNO building. The young boy finally made it home, but he got an ear infection and lifelong sinus problems for his trouble.

Sanchez, though his family was very poor, had some security in his father's employment for the railroad. Farmers fared worse, as their very livelihood was crippled by the lack of rain and relentless dust storms. Thousands of them loaded up their vehicles and moved west to California and Oregon, seeking work and more hospitable farming conditions.

Many Kansas farmers weathered the Dust Bowl, however. Some subsisted in part on government "commodities"—canned beef stew and other food rations—but most were proudly determined to live by their own means. Still, not even stubborn, hardworking farmers could get themselves out of the mess that was the Dust Bowl. Under President Franklin D. Roosevelt's "New Deal," more than nine thousand Kansas farmers received $1.3 million in aid in 1933. Nearly three hundred Public Works Administration projects—jobs created by the federal government to rejuvenate the economy—took place in the state over the course of five years. And the Works Progress Administration put many to work constructing buildings and runways or compiling a written and visual guide to Kansas. Some regretted seeking such assistance, but farmers and others had little choice.

The state itself had a libertarian streak and was reluctant to receive federal aid, even in the face of such disaster. But in April 1937, a state committee finally asked for help. Committee member H.A. Kinney, a businessman from Liberal, sent a telegram to President Franklin D. Roosevelt.

Drought conditions of the dust bowl have reached an emergency stage requiring desperate action. Stop. We appeal to the federal government for the preservation of life and property in the dust bowl area. Stop. Present program inadequate under individual operation to cover the area in time to accomplish necessary results. Stop. Work must be done under federal supervision working the soil with an army of tractors and listers planting seed with the first operation and covering the area systematically under orders beginning at the south and west sides of the dust bowl leaving no uncultivated land untouched until the entire area is covered. Stop. Imperative that the federal government declare an existing emergency and place martial law in effect throughout the dust bowl requiring immediate listing and planting. Stop. Blowing and shifting of the soil daily moving eastward at alarming rate. Stop. Concentrated and maximum effort vitally necessary to prevent utter destruction of the soil.

Eventually, rain returned to Kansas. But the years of its virtual absence left its mark on an entire generation of Kansans, their brows wrinkled from worry and the persistent sun. To avoid another crisis of blowing topsoil, the Soil Conservation Act of 1935 discouraged farming practices that caused soil erosion and taught farmers safer techniques for preserving fertile land. Kansas and the country hoped to avoid another devastating, perfect storm of drought, overworked land, and economic depression.

PLANES ON THE PLAINS

1944

Maybe it's the long, flat expanses of treeless prairie, a natural runway of sorts. Maybe it's the huge sky, unobstructed and impossible to ignore. Maybe it's the sense of confinement some might experience in a landlocked state, leading them to dream of escape into the clouds. Whatever the reason, Kansas—and, particularly, the town of Wichita—has a special history with flying.

In 1900, three years before the Wright brothers got off the ground, Carl Dryden Browne built a short-lived factory for commercial airplanes in Freedom, Kansas. Less than ten years later, two railroad mechanics in Goodland patented the first rotary-winged aircraft, an early prototype for the modern-day helicopter. In 1916, airplane designer Clyde Cessna moved his small-town operation in Kingman County to the big city of Wichita, where it would become Cessna Aircraft Company in 1928 and grow into one of the most successful companies in the world. Future aviation magnate Walter Beech also set up shop in Wichita around that time. And, of course, celebrity pilot Amelia Earhart hailed from Kansas. By the 1930s, Wichita was billing itself as "The Air Capital of the World."

Plenty of cities have their marginally true slogans aimed at self-promotion and economic development. But few could have predicted how true Wichita's "air capital" claim would become.

On the heels of the Great Depression, Kansas native Lloyd Stearman's aircraft company became a subsidiary of Seattle-based Boeing Airplane Company in 1938. Then, when World War II broke out, Boeing landed the federal government contract to produce B-29 bombers for the United States military. The final groundwork had been laid for an aviation revolution in Wichita.

The numbers tell the story of Wichita's aviation boom. In 1938, Wichita factories produced three hundred planes. Compare that with the twenty-six thousand aircraft they pumped out over the next few years, as the war raged and the military industrial complex swung into gear (in Kansas as a whole, the number was an impressive 34,500). Boeing produced the B-29 bomber, while Beech built AT-10 and AT-11 bomber trainers, and Cessna crafted the twin-engined T-50 Bobcat.

The U.S. government moved in, building military air bases throughout the state—safely nestled in the heart of the country, away from vulnerable coastlines—and giving contracts to local companies poised to meet demand. Wichita's Coleman Company, for instance, was hired to manufacture portable stoves, ammunition chests, and shell casings for soldiers. Culver Aircraft Corporation, contracted under complete secrecy, built radio-controlled drones. Ultimately, the state nabbed almost $3 billion in war contracts, and Wichita had the highest number of war contracts per capita in the nation. In 1942 alone, more than $2 billion in defense spending was funneled into Wichita. In 1939, 3 percent of Wichitans worked for aircraft companies but, by 1943, sixty thousand of them—half of all Wichita employees—did so, on a collective $9 million payroll; the town was rivaled only by San Diego in its industrial growth. Neighboring small towns enjoyed increased commerce as bomber pilots utilized their modest runways for training purposes. Official army airfields popped up across the state, and naval air stations were constructed in Hutchinson and Olathe.

The Great Depression was over. Money was moving, airplanes were being built, and people were back to work.

Those people were, in part, Kansas farmers. Destitute after the Depression, they put their knowledge of machinery and tools, plus their tremendous work ethic, to work in the factories. In 1942, half of the workers at the Boeing plant in Wichita had farming backgrounds, and many of them continued to produce wheat and other crops while producing B-29 bombers. For their extra toil, their income more than doubled.

Sturdy Kansas farmer-types—most of whom were white—gave much to the war effort, but with the youngest and healthiest sent overseas to join the frontlines, Wichita's factories needed to broaden their concept of the American worker. In the earliest period of the war, African Americans were only hired by aircraft factories to mop floors and clean bathrooms. But, by 1943, the companies began hiring African Americans for the assembly line and other positions. Women, too, ascended the ranks; once brought into the fold to squeeze into the small crevices of airplanes on the assembly line, soon they worked at many phases of production, most commonly tightening rivets that fastened one airplane piece to another. In 1946, women composed half of Boeing workers, and 40 percent of Beech workers, in Wichita.

Still, even a diverse local workforce could not keep up with the race to equip the military, known within the aviation industry as "the Battle of Kansas." Workers began pouring into Wichita from all corners of the country, seeking good-paying jobs and bringing with them their families and myriad cultural backgrounds. The Wichita population leapt from 114,634 in 1940 to 133,011 in 1941. In 1942, nearly 200,000 people called the Wichita metropolitan area home. At the center of it all, in the giant, sparkling, light-filled factory buildings, whites, blacks, women, and geographic transplants all worked together to achieve industrial feats. Together, they won the wartime "Battle of Kansas," quickly shaving the worker hours needed to build a B-29 bomber from 157,000 to 57,000.

Transformed into a bustling industrial mecca overnight, the city of Wichita hurried to catch up with its opportunity. The city hired a traffic consultant to devise new signs, parking meters, and other devices to control the seemingly endless rivers of cars moving through town. Stores and restaurants stayed open twenty-four hours a day to accommodate workers on all three shifts at the factories, which also operated all night long. Child care services, public transportation, movie theaters—all of them were open around the clock. Boeing became the first manufacturer in the country to use mass transportation for its workers; buses moved tens of thousands of employees from downtown Wichita, Arkansas City, Winfield, Salina, Ponca City, and Newkirk to the Boeing assembly lines and back. Elderly locals who remembered Wichita as a dusty cow town in the late nineteenth century must have felt their heads spinning.

When housing needs became an issue, the government paid for the construction of thousands of new houses for aviation workers. They were organized into three communities: Beechwood, Hilltop Manor, and the largest, Planeview, aptly named for its proximity to Boeing on the south side of Wichita.

Planeview alone boasted 4,328 new houses and within a year of its establishment was at full capacity, its residents hailing from forty-two states. Planeview had its own police department, fire department, shops, grocery store, and combined junior high and high school of nearly two thousand students. For the many families who had struggled and starved during the Great Depression, this land of brand-new ovens, green lawns, and steady employment was known as "the Miracle City." At the end of the war, Planeview was the seventh largest city in Kansas and, with its like communities, served as a prototype of sorts for the well-manicured suburban developments that would blossom across the country in the 1950s.

With the war's end came another sudden shift for Wichita. Jobs disappeared as quickly as they had materialized, with Boeing once laying off sixteen thousand employees in one day. So too would the government-built, wartime housing disappear. But World War II and the related boom in the aviation industry forever changed the Wichita landscape.

Its population had nearly doubled, as sixty-seven thousand people moved to Sedgwick County, drawn mostly by the airplane factories, during the war. The face of the town was more racially and ethnically diverse, owing to that influx of new residents from every corner of the country. The women of Wichita had enjoyed a taste of careers outside the home. The local economy was strong. Wichita aircraft manufacturers were known around the globe and in coming decades would adapt to societal needs, applying their production capabilities to commercial airplanes and business jets. Wichita had made good on its claim of being the Air Capital of the World.

MENTAL REVOLUTION

1953

For the first half of the twentieth century, the Kansas mental health care system was in a bad place. The state's mental hospitals were dismal places where the mentally ill were stowed away, to be hidden from society and to receive only the most basic services, such as food and housing, until they died and were forgotten in the hospital cemeteries.

In the late 1940s, when the state system ranked last in the nation, the Kansas legislature got serious about turning things around. And they knew there was but one man for the job: Dr. Karl Menninger.

Menninger was a world-renowned psychiatrist in their midst, a progressive mental health specialist who had established an innovative private practice with his father and brother, right there in the capital city of Topeka. Menninger accepted the task and, with $21 million from the state, revolutionized the Kansas mental health care system in a handful of years, improving care and turning the state mental hospital in Topeka into a world-class teaching institution. Thousands of patients now lived in comfortable, caring environments in which they could improve rather than dark dungeons in which they could only deteriorate.

In 1953, Karl's brother, Dr. Will Menninger, traveled the country explaining the turnaround to legislators in twenty-eight states, all the while championing funding for state treatments of mental illness. The Menningers' secret to successful treatment was simple. They viewed the mentally ill as individuals, human beings who were the products of their environments, rather than shameful miscreants who were best kept in shadows. At the time, such an idea was revolutionary, and lawmakers across the country were eager to re-envision their state mental health facilities with the Menninger philosophy. The philosophy was honed by Karl and Will but owed much to the influence of their father, who died the same year of Will's historic speaking tour of state capitals.

Karl and Will came from a home in which deep concern for the disadvantaged was a way of life. Their father, Charles, was a country doctor and a professor at Campbell University, a small college in Holton; he and wife Flora were generous members of the community. When a massive flood destroyed nearby North Topeka in 1903, when Karl was six, the Menningers took several newly homeless people into their home.

A few years later, in 1908, Charles visited the new Mayo Clinic in Minnesota and was impressed with the idea that a family of physicians could band together in a cohesive treatment program. He declared to Karl and Will, his oldest and youngest sons, that they would be doctors, and that the Menningers would open a family-run clinic in Topeka. The boys were mere children, but their father's dream came to fruition.

Karl grew up to attend Washburn University in Topeka, Indiana University, and the University of Wisconsin, where he graduated in 1914. He then graduated from Harvard Medical School in 1917 and served in the Naval Reserve during World War I before working under mentor Dr. Ernest Southard at the Boston Psychopathic Hospital and teaching neuropathology at Harvard Medical School. He returned to Topeka to open a practice with his father, and he brought with him his unexpected turn toward psychiatry.

Karl and father Charles co-founded the Menninger Clinic in 1919 on the outskirts of Topeka in an old farmhouse with beds for thirteen patients. They viewed the clinic as a holistic environment in which patients would receive exercise, visits from specialists, and, most importantly, a sense that they were among family. Charles theorized that no patient was untreatable, and together the Menningers made good on that promise. Within five years, they opened the Menninger Sanitarium, and in 1926 they founded the Southard School aimed at treating psychologically troubled children. The Menninger operation flourished with its residential approach, ultimately growing to thirty-nine buildings on 430 acres, with a staff of nine hundred. By 1941, the clinic and sanitarium were recognized among the top in the country and became the not-for-profit Menninger Foundation. Karl's first book, *The Human Mind*, published in 1930, was the first book on mental health written in layman's terms and became a bestseller. He continued his crossover appeal by writing a column on child-rearing for *Household* magazine from 1929 to 1942 and an advice column for *Ladies' Home Journal* from 1930 to 1932. These efforts, combined with his academic writings, helped dispel stereotypes about troubled individuals written off as "lunatics."

In the meantime, Karl had steeped himself in Sigmund Freud's theories on psychoanalysis. He received the first certificate awarded by the Chicago Psychoanalytic Institute. In 1942, Karl and brother William opened the Topeka Institute for Psychoanalysis, though they expounded on Freud's therapy-session model by considering individuals' total environments beyond the patient's couch.

When Karl returned from assessing the psychiatric needs of World War II soldiers in Europe, he became manager of Winter Hospital, the country's largest Veterans Administration hospital, in Topeka. Contracting with the government, the Menningers developed a psychiatric residency program there, opening the Menninger School of Psychiatry in 1946. During the postwar years, the school trained half of all Veterans Administration psychiatrists and more than a third of all psychiatric residents in the country—leaving its Freudian mark on a whopping 15 percent of all working American psychiatrists. The Menningers also developed at the hospital a doctoral program in clinical psychology, funded by the National Institutes of Mental Health.

As they led psychiatry into a new era, in which mental troubles and even criminal acts might be viewed as the result of parental abuses or society's failings rather than individual failures, the Menningers continued to take care to create a caring, productive environment for all patients.

"It should be a help for any people to be getting three square meals a day," Karl Menninger said, "and to know that there is opportunity ahead—things to be done, land to be turned, things to build."

Much of the psychiatric profession, however, continued practices the Menningers viewed as barbaric, such as electroshock therapy—the administration of electric currents through the brain, during which patients might convulse, foam at the mouth, and soil themselves. This "somatic" approach was derived from the idea that illnesses such as schizophrenia were physical, not mental in nature. "Psychodynamic" psychiatrists such as the Menningers, meanwhile, viewed depression and other disorders as strictly mental conditions in most cases and railed against the use of electroshock therapy.

In 1946, Will Menninger helped found the Group for the Advancement of Psychiatry (GAP), which called upon the American

Psychiatric Association (APA) to modernize the profession; GAP's first report of the state of psychiatry was a blistering attack on the "indiscriminate" use of electroshock therapy, particularly its use in private office settings and for a wide variety of diagnoses. Meanwhile, Karl chaired a committee to reorganize the APA and squelched electroshock treatments when called upon to fix the ailing Kansas mental health care system.

In their own now world-famous treatment center, which drew leading mental health professionals from around the world, Karl served as chief of staff, constantly reexamining therapeutic approaches. "What do we know?" he would ask in his fiery manner at staff meetings. "How can we be sure?" Will, a quieter presence, handled more organizational matters before dying in 1966.

Karl lived a long life and remained prolific in his work. The year of Will's death, Karl founded The Villages, a group home for homeless children in Topeka. In 1978, at the age of eighty-five, he co-directed a federal initiative on programs and housing for Native American tribes in the Southwest. He gave electric lectures on criminology, mental hygiene, and abnormal psychiatry at Washburn University in Topeka. His major books after *The Human Mind* included *Love Against Hate,* on which he collaborated with second wife Jeanetta Lyle, in 1959; *Man Against Himself,* an examination of suicide, in 1956; *The Crime of Punishment,* which accused the prison system of being ineffective and cruel and resulted in many institutional reforms, in 1968; and *Whatever Became of Sin?* in 1988.

Karl became a close acquaintance of Dr. Anna Freud, Sigmund Freud's daughter, with whom he shared an interest in child psychiatry. In 1981, he received the nation's highest civilian honor, the Medal of Freedom, from President Jimmy Carter.

In his later years, Karl Menninger was even more convinced of the power of environment on the shaping of behavior and thus championed healthy parenting practices and even the "promotion" of top high school teachers to elementary classrooms, where they might do the most good.

"Most of my life has been spent in treating persons one by one," Menninger said. "But as I become increasingly aware of the extent of misery and hopelessness in our society, I think more of preventing unnecessary suffering at the source, before individuals take or are forced to take the wrong road."

Menninger died of abdominal cancer in 1990, just shy of his ninety-seventh birthday and by then known as the "dean of American psychiatry." The Menninger psychiatric center maintained its family roots, as Karl's and Will's sons took over where their fathers left off. In 2003, after eighty-four years in Topeka, the clinic moved to Houston, Texas.

SEPARATE BUT NOT EQUAL

1954

On an autumn day, Oliver Brown walked his seven-year-old daughter, Linda, up the steps to the front door of Sumner Elementary School. The school was for white children, but Brown was determined to attempt to enroll his black daughter there. Sumner was just seven blocks from their Topeka home. Linda should have the right to attend school there, he reasoned. It would be much simpler than her current situation, which involved walking several blocks to board a bus to Monroe Elementary, one of the capital city's four all-black schools, a mile across town.

Brown stepped through the doors of the white school and talked with the white secretary. She sent him into the white principal's office, while daughter Linda waited outside. Loud voices boomed through the closed door. Then, Brown exited the inner office, took his daughter by the hand and left. Linda had been denied enrollment to the school.

It was the early 1950s. Brown made his living as a welder for the Santa Fe Railroad and was a leader within his community, serving as assistant pastor at an area church and providing for a cohesive, loving family. But the administrators at Sumner Elementary didn't care about any of that. They saw the dark shade of his skin and turned him and little Linda away.

Brown knew that would happen, of course. The entire event had been planned, part of a national movement to desegregate the public school system.

It was a system of racial discrimination that operated legally in the wake of a landmark, 1896 United States Supreme Court decision, *Plessy v. Ferguson*, in which the court ruled that separate, discriminatory public institutions were constitutional, so long as each provided the same services: in other words, "separate but equal." The reality of segregated public education, of course, was that separate white and black schools were far from equal. Black children often faced dismal learning environments of outdated textbooks, insufficient supplies, leaking ceilings, and crumbling walls.

Black schools in Topeka were of higher quality than those in other parts of the country but, for Linda Brown, the thought of attending Sumner Elementary was about more than educational opportunity. It meant going to class with the same little girls she had befriended in her own neighborhood. Her friends were a mix of ethnicities, but their lighter skin meant they could attend Sumner.

"We lived in an integrated neighborhood and I had all of these playmates of different nationalities. And so when I found out that day that I might be able to go to their school, I was just thrilled, you know," Brown would remember as an adult. Being turned away from Sumner was a confusing experience for her. "I just couldn't understand what was happening because I was so sure that I was going to go to school with Mona and Guinevere, Wanda, and all of my playmates."

Her father had staged the doomed enrollment attempt under the direction of the National Association for the Advancement of

Colored People (NAACP), whose mission he'd been convinced to join. The organization had courted him, knowing that such a model citizen would make an ideal plaintiff in a social climate given to racial stereotypes and general fear of black people. Other black parents across the state joined the charge, and their children's documented experiences of institutionalized discrimination laid the groundwork for a class-action lawsuit that would challenge the lawfulness of segregation.

The case, *Oliver Brown et al. v. The Board of Education of Topeka, Kansas,* happened to utilize Brown's name but involved twelve other plaintiffs in the state: Darlene Brown, Lena Carper, Sadie Emmanuel, Marguerite Emerson, Shirley Fleming, Zelma Henderson, Shirley Hodison, Maude Lawton, Alma Lewis, Iona Richardson, and Lucinda Todd, on behalf of their twenty children. The District Court, citing *Plessy v. Ferguson*, ruled in favor of the Board of Education. Its decision acknowledged disadvantage among black children in a segregated school system but insisted that black and white Topeka schools were of equal quality and therefore lawful.

Eventually, the lawsuit made its way to the Supreme Court. By the time it got there, it was merged with similar cases in South Carolina (*Briggs v. Elliott*), Washington, D.C. (*Bolling v. Sharpe*), Delaware (*Gebhart v. Belton*), and Virginia (*Davis v. County School Board of Prince Edward County*), where sixteen-year-old Barbara Rose Johns had whipped up a 450-student walkout at Moton High School. The NAACP, which filed the suits, organized all of them under the Kansas case's name in the hope that the state's abolitionist history would help their cause. Also, the relatively good state of black schools in Topeka meant that the court would have to focus on factors beyond the physical conditions of schools and examine the intangible implications and psychological woes of segregation.

The strategy paid off. Following masterful arguments by NAACP chief counsel Thurgood Marshall, who would later serve as a Supreme Court justice, and an unimpassioned state defense by assistant attorney general Paul Wilson, who would become a distinguished emeritus professor of law at the University of Kansas, the Supreme Court obliterated the "separate but equal" doctrine by ruling unanimously in favor of the plaintiffs on May 17, 1954.

"In these days, it is doubtful that any child may reasonably be expected to succeed in life if he is denied the opportunity of an education," read the court decision. "Such an opportunity . . . is a right which must be made available to all on equal terms. . . . Does segregation of children in public schools solely on the basis of race, even though the physical facilities and other 'tangible' factors may be equal, deprive the children of the minority group of equal educational opportunities? We believe that it does. . . . We conclude that in the field of public education the doctrine of 'separate but equal' has no place. Separate educational facilities are inherently unequal."

Legal segregation of public schools had come to an end.

Back in Topeka, change already was underway. Two elementary school districts were integrated in August 1953, and the rest of the districts joined the charge after the 1954 decision. No demonstrations of record disrupted the efforts, perhaps because Topeka middle schools had been integrated since 1941, and Topeka High School had been integrated since it was established in 1871. Racism was pervasive, but real change was afoot.

The *Brown v. Board of Education* decision didn't go over quite as well elsewhere. Virginia senator Harry Byrd led a major backlash, preferring to close schools rather than let black children through their doors. Arkansas governor Orval Faubus used National Guardsmen to keep nine black students from entering Little Rock High School, until President Dwight D. Eisenhower—a Kansas native—protected the students' admission with federal troops. The Arkansas youth, who would be known as the "Little Rock Nine," faced hateful taunts and threats as they entered the high school.

Today, the hardships faced by the Little Rock Nine and other minority youth are brought to life at the Brown v. Board of Education National Historic Site—housed in the building of old Monroe Elementary School, the black school in Topeka attended by Linda Brown. The museum, operated by the National Park Service, also pays tribute to the landmark court decision's Kansas connections and is in large part the result of efforts by Cheryl Brown Henderson—Linda's sister—to establish Monroe Elementary as a National Historic Site. The 1920s school building, today surrounded by huge trees and a smattering of old, brick warehouses, was reborn as a historical learning site in 2004, marking the fiftieth anniversary of *Brown v. Board*, and each year hosts about thirty thousand visitors from all over the world. Old photographs, documents, and recordings are mixed in with the child-sized water fountains from which young Linda Brown drank before her last name became part of what's thought by many to be the most important Supreme Court decision in United States history.

Brown Henderson, who was three years old when her father's case was settled, wrote to commemorate the decision's fiftieth anniversary.

"We should pay particular attention to the Brown decision, because of the weight placed on its importance by legal scholars and historians alike," Brown Henderson wrote. "With Brown, the high court issued a definitive interpretation of the fourteenth amendment to our Constitution, making it clear that every individual in this country was entitled to 'equal protection under the laws' without regard to race, ethnicity, gender, disability, age or any other circumstance."

PIECE OF THE PIE

1958

Brothers Frank and Dan Carney learned about small-business values from their father. He disliked working for Cudahy Packing Company, believing it was too large to properly tend to its employees and products. So he quit.

The boys' father bought a corner grocery store on a main road in Wichita. The small environment, with few employees and a direct link to the community, was right up his alley. He taught teenaged Frank and Dan how to run the place—ordering shipments, stocking shelves, assisting customers. Then, the small-businessman died, leaving his wife and two sons to take care of the corner store.

Frank and Dan worked at the store into their college years at Wichita State University. It was a straightforward, quiet job, but down the street, things were raucous. A tiny building, with a roof reminiscent of a hut, housed an unsavory drinking establishment where truckers regularly got drunk and loud. Fights would erupt from time to time, and on at least one occasion a surly trucker wandered into a proper ladies' tearoom across the street. The owners of the building were tired of dealing with the unruly business, B & B Lounge. They wanted to be done with the bar but needed to collect rent; the building owners approached the hardworking brothers down the street. Would they consider opening a quiet little restaurant there?

The Carney brothers were intrigued with the opportunity. But they didn't want to open up the usual hamburger joint. They wanted to serve something unique, something Wichitans couldn't get anywhere else.

Someone showed the brothers a recent *Saturday Evening Post* article about an eating fad taking New York City by storm: pizza. Italian immigrants had been making pizza there for decades. But when World War II soldiers returned from Italy singing the praises of cheese-and-tomato-filled pizza, Americans finally began to take notice. "The highly seasoned pizza with its tough crust and tomato topping is such a gastronomical craze that the open pie threatens the pre-eminence of the hot dog and hamburger," the *New York Times* reported in 1953.

The Carneys wanted a piece of the action.

First, they borrowed $600 from their mother. Next, they rounded up an old oven and a plastic baby bathtub—in which to mix pizza dough. They got a lesson in pizza-making from a local, and their mom sewed curtains from red-and-white checkered fabric. Now, they just needed a name.

When a family member commented that the tiny building resembled a hut, they had their business name: Pizza Hut. It was simple, apt, and, conveniently, fit on the sign used by the defunct B&B Lounge.

At the ages of nineteen and twenty-four, the brothers opened their unusual restaurant on June 15, 1958. Knowing that many Wichitans might be dubious about pizza, they gave away slices to entice new customers.

Soon, demand for their cheesy pies was more than they'd hoped for, with cars streaming into their parking lot from the busy intersection of Kellogg and Bluff Streets. The handles melted off their old oven as they raced to keep up with the hungry crowds, and within weeks the brothers were pulling in a thousand dollars a week.

A year later, the Carney brothers had five Pizza Huts in Wichita and had incorporated their business. They opened franchises in Topeka and across Kansas—careful to replicate their red-roofed original—soon crossing state lines into Oklahoma and Texas. In 1968, just a decade after opening their first Pizza Hut in Wichita, Pizza Hut had made its way to Canada and was an international brand. Franchises popped up in Europe and Australia and, by 1971, Pizza Hut was the world's top pizza chain, with more restaurant locations and higher sales than any other. The next year, the company went public and was traded on the New York Stock Exchange.

Dan and Frank were very rich men. But something wasn't quite right.

Pizza Hut was huge—too huge, perhaps. The Kansas brothers were becoming disenchanted with their self-made empire. They were detached from the daily operations of their business, and their jobs bore little resemblance to the days of shoving pizzas into an old oven on a street in Wichita. Just as their father had left a good job at a large packing company, the Carney brothers would leave their positions atop a major world corporation.

Dan left the company in 1974. Then, in 1977, stockholders approved a merger with Pepsico, Inc., for a reported $300 million. Pepsico maintained Pizza Hut's corporate headquarters in Wichita, but Frank couldn't hold on any longer. He left the company in 1980.

The Pizza Hut headquarters left Wichita for Dallas in 1995, and the company continued to dominate the world fast-food market. By the new millennium, it had yet another new owner and ten thousand restaurants, almost a third of which were located in eighty-six foreign countries.

Meanwhile, while Dan became involved in the hotel industry, Frank moved on to Chi-Chi's Mexican restaurants before causing a stink by endorsing a Pizza Hut rival, Papa John's Pizza.

Pizza Hut has moved a long way from its humble Wichita origins, but the original "hut" building was moved to the Wichita State University campus, where it was preserved as a monument to entrepreneurialism.

SHOTGUN ARTIST

1981–1997

Some of the greatest creative minds of the twentieth century were born and raised in Kansas: painter Aaron Douglas, photographer Gordon Parks, playwright William Inge. While these individuals eventually left the Sunflower State, one artistic icon actually moved in, long after he found fame and acclaim.

William S. Burroughs became a counterculture hero with the publication of his groundbreaking novel *Naked Lunch* in 1959. The book, brimming with sex and violence, was banned in the United States in 1962, cementing Burroughs's reputation as a beatnik legend. Burroughs, with fellow "Beats" Jack Kerouac and Allen Ginsberg, spent the 1940s and '50s hitchhiking, creating art, and experimenting with drugs. Burroughs's reckless lifestyle culminated in the untimely death of his wife at a drug-fueled party in Mexico; Burroughs attempted to shoot a wine glass off her head and instead killed her. The tragedy was the impetus for a celebrated literary career, as Burroughs funneled his experiences into creative expression.

Burroughs would live in London, New York, Paris, and Tangier. Eventually, though, he lost interest in big-city life; at the age of sixty-seven, Burroughs followed friend and romantic partner James Grauerholz to Lawrence, Kansas, in 1981. Two years later, he became a writer-in-residence at the University of Kansas, located in Lawrence.

The relocation shocked other literary powerhouses—Kansas? But he insisted the move was no detriment to his art. Indeed, Burroughs lost nothing when he left the bright lights behind.

"My working habits are about the same in Lawrence as they were in New York," Burroughs told an interviewer in 1987. "I didn't go to parties or discotheques. I've never been to Studio 54. I didn't go to various celebrity in-spots."

He far preferred Lawrence, where he could "get out of doors and row, and shoot, and keep cats, and things that I can't do in New York." Burroughs—free-thinking author, counterculture homosexual, former heroin addict—had found a home in Kansas. Once famous for moving restlessly, as was the beatnik way, the author was happier gardening in his backyard. He wasn't exactly a docile old man, though. In his Lawrence home, the tall, gaunt author guzzled vodka-and-colas and kept a sharp blade hidden inside his walking cane.

Burroughs may have slowed down, but his creative work didn't. He continued his efforts as a writer, publishing *Cities of the Red Night* (1981), *The Place of Dead Roads* (1983), and *The Western Lands* (1987). And he found a highly innovative way to make a painting.

Burroughs discovered that the unpredictable art of abstract painting became even more exciting when firearms were involved. Sometimes collaborating with Grauerholz, Burroughs would go to a friend's property outside of town, place cans of spray paint in front of plywood or old doors, aim his gun and—splat. The results were hole-ridden wood marked by violent splashes of color; he called the works "shotgun art." The work found its way to the London and

New York art scenes, where it caused a sensation. But, for Burroughs, his only aim was to realize his own vision.

And what a unique vision it was. In the early phase of his experiments with guns and spray paint, Burroughs related the seemingly simple process to the "perceptual shifts" he experienced throughout his life, including apparent hallucinations of little gray men and green reindeer.

"If you see something, it's a shift of vision, not a hallucination," Burroughs said. "You shift your vision. What you see is there, but you have to be in a certain place to see it. I think everyone has one or two of these experiences at one time or another. I think an actual shift of vision is involved. I'm doing some pure chance paintings now that seem to produce these perceptual shifts. For example, you take a piece of plywood and a spray-paint can and stand back and shoot the can with a shotgun. The can explodes—it will go thirty feet. Now you look at this thing and there's a shift. You can see all kinds of things in there. Movies, little scenes, streets. Anybody can see it. They're there somewhere."

Members of Burroughs's "Beat" generation had drifted from place to place, always moving, and their writing was similarly disjointed. So it only made sense that Burroughs's visual art was concerned with the idea of motion. Setting paint flying at explosive speed was one means of achieving motion on the canvas.

"If you sit in front of something and paint it, that's one thing; but if you try and paint what you see when you're moving, you're going to be creating a totally different landscape," Burroughs said. "You can't put that moving, perceptual landscape—particularly urban phenomena—down on a canvas using the old representational methods."

Burroughs continued to mix bullets and art for years. By 1996, with nearly a decade of paint-blasting under his belt, he viewed the process as an act of liberation.

"The shotgun blast releases the little spirits compacted into the layers of wood, releases the colors of the paints to splash out in unforeseen images and patterns," Burroughs wrote to a reporter.

The writer had become a visual artist, and he still had a few tricks up his sleeve.

Kurt Cobain, the lead singer for grunge-rock icon Nirvana, deeply admired Burroughs's writing and approached him about collaborating on a record. In 1992, Burroughs recorded a short story in his old, gravelly voice at his Lawrence home, and the reading was mixed with Cobain's guitar riffs, recorded elsewhere. The result was "The 'Priest' They Called Him," about a heroin junkie who dies on Christmas Eve. Burroughs was addicted to heroin for much of his life; Cobain battled heroin addiction until he shot himself in 1994. In the brief period between the collaboration and the suicide, though, Cobain traveled to Lawrence to exchange gifts and spend time with the elderly Burroughs in his home.

Cobain envisioned Burroughs playing a major role in the video for the Nirvana song "Heart-Shaped Box." He described his vision for the music video in his posthumously published journals, demonstrating through symbols his desire to carry on Burroughs's anti-establishment artistry: "William and I sitting across from one another at a table (black and white) lots of Blinding Sun from the windows behind us holding hands staring into each others eyes. He gropes me from behind and falls dead on top of me. Medical footage of sperm flowing through penis. A ghost vapor comes out of his chest and groin area and enters me Body [sic]." Burroughs declined the acting invitation, and another old man was used for the video.

Burroughs collaborated with other artists, including alternative rock group R.E.M.; for the 1996 album *Songs in the Key of X: Music from and Inspired by the X-Files,* he offered a spoken-word version of the band's previously recorded "Star Me Kitten."

Burroughs forged relationships with other musicians, including Blondie's Deborah Harry, and he continued to make visual art. He revived his "shotgun art" for a 1995 collaboration series with English artist Ralph Steadman, famous for illustrating Hunter S. Thompson's *Fear and Loathing in Las Vegas.* Steadman admired Burroughs's splatter-paintings when they were shown in London in the 1980s, and he traveled to Lawrence for the new project. Together, Burroughs and Steadman created a series of images entitled *And Something New Has Been Added,* which involved Steadman's etching of Burroughs's face, placed on either side of a bulls-eye. Then, of course, Burroughs took aim with a gun. The series included a print for each of Burroughs's eighty-two years.

A London writer described the Lawrence meeting between the two celebrated artists as being something of a circus: "swarms of assistants, acolytes, relatives, parasites, somebody taping the whole thing on video, another person with a Leica, flunkies tripping over each other. Burroughs, bent double as he is, retains a jerky, restless vigour, riffling through the prints Steadman has brought along, pulling revolvers out of his pocket and demonstrating the workings of the safety mechanisms, steadily chugging on a long beaker of vodka and Coke that is regularly replenished." During the meeting, the typically gruff Burroughs was delighted to see a print of Steadman's entitled *Nostalgia for the Future,* showing people floating around in a futuristic setting; the painting was inspired by one of Burroughs's books.

In August 1997, after sixteen eventful years as a Kansan, Burroughs had a heart attack and died in Lawrence at the age of eighty-three.

CITY DIVIDED

1991

Every day, around 7:00 a.m., they arrive by car and bus. They are sweaty; the summer heat is powerful even at the early hour. Dozens of them, carrying signs, approach an unremarkable Wichita building on a major thoroughfare. Their signs read STOP THE KILLING or SAVE THE BABIES and include graphic images of aborted fetuses. Together, they congregate around the entrance to Women's Health Care Services, an abortion clinic operated by Dr. George Tiller.

For forty-two days, beginning in mid-July, the protest— termed the "Summer of Mercy" by organizing anti-abortion group Operation Rescue—deeply divided the city of about three hundred thousand people. Some Wichitans honked in approval as they passed the protesters, who spent hours praying outside the clinic—praying the Rosary, reading from Bibles, and loudly denouncing abortion. Other locals spoke out against Operation Rescue's more aggressive tactics, which included blocking patients from entering the clinic and yelling threats as Dr. Tiller entered his practice each morning.

Throughout Operation Rescue's protest, a smaller and less organized group of pro-choice advocates could be found across the street, holding signs reading ABORT OPERATION RESCUE. But the anti-abortion demonstration, organized on a national level, drew all the attention. Network television news broadcasted video of protesters using their bodies to block access to Tiller's clinic and lying on the asphalt parking lot to stop cars from entering. U.S. District Judge Patrick Kelly issued an order against the group's actions, and the U.S. Marshal Service produced barricades to maintain distance between the protesters and the clinic. In return, some protesters attempted to cross the barricades or scale fences to access the clinic's main entrance. Members of the Wichita police department worked hundreds of hours of overtime, arresting twenty-six hundred people in just over a month, wielding batons, and using Mace to control unruly individuals. In some recorded instances, officers arrested their pastors, brothers-in-law, or friends. Local radio shows and newspapers were in a frenzy, reporters covering every angle of the event and residents calling or writing in with their concerns and strong opinions. Some locals used vacation time at work to participate in the protest. Many who had never made any kind of stir, let alone gotten in trouble with the law, spent time in jail and acquired rap sheets. In a single day, eighty Catholic priests were among those arrested. Wichita had become the epicenter of one of the most controversial issues of the time: abortion.

"The continued protests threaten to shred the community's social fabric," read an editorial in the *Wichita Eagle*. "Neighbor is being pitted against neighbor, workplace colleague against workplace colleague, church member against church member. At risk is the sense of community togetherness that makes Wichita more than a collection of houses and businesses."

Indeed, the national debate played out in the lives of Wichitans that summer. One Wichita woman, who worked as Tiller's spokeswoman, had a teenage son; her son happened to date a girl who participated in the Operation Rescue protests. The young couple was a microcosm of the divide going on in the country and in Wichita—the boy's mother was pro-choice, while the girl's mother had been arrested twice in an antiabortion protest.

Another Wichitan, a small businessman in his forties, counted the antiabortion protest as his first demonstration of any kind. On one occasion, he joined other protesters in sitting around Tiller's car, as the doctor attempted to enter the clinic; the stranded Tiller waited at length for police to clear a path. (Though unprecedented in scope, the protest was a familiar climate for Tiller, disdained by many for performing third-trimester abortions; his one-story, wood-paneled building amid small shops and car dealerships was blown open by a pipe bomb in 1986.)

Numerous patients experienced the protests on a very personal level, hiding their faces as they passed through the loud, disapproving crowd.

A college sophomore from Kansas helped them enter the clinic, on one occasion making the local television news in a T-shirt from the Kansas Prochoice Action League; when relatives saw her on TV, they stopped speaking to her.

The wild scene involved more than just Kansans.

One woman, a middle-aged science teacher from New Jersey, wriggled under police barricades to block the front entrance to the abortion clinic and, on at least one occasion, wriggled out of handcuffs.

An Ohio man was arrested on the sidewalk outside the clinic for proclaiming that God would strike down Tiller; Judge Kelly dismissed the charges, deeming the incident not a threat but an expression protected by the First Amendment.

However, the federal judge was none too pleased with the overall scene at Tiller's clinic. When he dispatched marshals to the clinic, he warned that anyone who disobeyed his order not to block the clinic entrance "should say farewell to their family and bring their tooth-brush, and I mean it, because they're going to jail."

The heat at the abortion clinic spread into the channels of the U.S. government when the Justice Department, under President George Bush, attempted to step in and halt Judge Kelly's order. The judge denounced the administration's actions on national television.

Some antiabortion protesters identified Judge Kelly as a villain of sorts for interfering with their attempts to seal off the clinic. Orga-nizers described his court order and the resultant arrests as "tyranny" and "Gestapo-style terrorist tactics," though the 10th U.S. Circuit Court of Appeals upheld Kelly's injunction. The judge encountered angry individuals on his front lawn, received several death threats, and was assigned a twenty-four-hour security detail. Kelly attempted to round up protest leaders on conspiracy charges, but at least one of them fled the state.

Wichitans were beginning to tire of the madness. The city had spent more than $400,000 on police overtime and other law-enforcement costs (in addition to about $150,000 spent by the county and nearly $300,000 spent by the U.S. Marshals Service). Residents near the protest site complained that their children couldn't sleep, due to noise occurring well into the night. Signs popped up in Wichita yards telling Operation Rescue to go home. For some, it was no longer about the issue of abortion but about returning to normalcy. Even the antiabortion mayor expressed a desire for the city to move on.

The crowd outside Tiller's clinic, which had peaked at more than one thousand individuals, began to dwindle. Leaders hinted that they would wrap things up and, to mark their departure, organized a massive rally in late August. About twenty-five thousand people filled the football stadium of Wichita State University to rally against abortion, using umbrellas to shield themselves from the sun on a one-hundred-degree day. Then Operation Rescue left town, for the most part.

George Tiller's clinic, however, did not escape future protest, and violent extremists continued to target the place. In 1993, Tiller was shot in each arm while leaving the clinic; a woman was convicted and sent to prison, and Tiller returned to his practice. Five years later, the clinic received an anthrax threat, later determined to be a hoax. In 2001, protesters showed up to mark the ten-year anniversary of the "Summer of Mercy." Then, in June 2009, Tiller was shot and killed by an antiabortion gunman while attending Sunday services at his church in Wichita. The murder was denounced by members of both sides of the abortion debate.

GATEWAY TO HELL

1993

Pope John Paul II, en route to the massive 1993 gathering of Catholics in Denver, Colorado, gave the pilot an order: Take a detour and avoid flying over northeast Kansas. The pope knew that the area was home to a wee town called Stull—no less than one of the world's seven gateways to hell. *Time* magazine even questioned the pope about his curious flight path, circumventing Kansas rather than flying straight over it into adjacent Colorado. The pope replied that he didn't want to fly over unholy ground.

At least that's how the story goes.

Of course, the *Time* magazine article never existed, and Pope John Paul II may never have heard of Stull, Kansas. But the tale is enduring and pervasive, known both to Kansans and enthusiasts for the paranormal worldwide.

Stull is a tiny dot on the landscape, barely laying claim to the title of "town." Settled in 1856 as Deer Creek Community, the place is comprised of a few houses, a church, and a handful of residents. The name "Stull" has been on the map since 1899, honoring former postmaster Sylvester Stull, though the town hasn't had a post office since 1903. It's an inconspicuous place, almost invisible, really. Yet it has achieved national or even worldwide infamy among pagans and the occult. This feat owes much, perhaps, to Stull's proximity to the town of Lawrence—home to the University of Kansas and plenty of thrill-seeking college students.

In November 1974, KU's college newspaper, the *University Daily Kansan,* reported that Stull was believed to be a center of supernatural activity. But the supposed activity wasn't your run-of-the-mill ghost lady in a white dress or predictable spirit of a Civil War soldier. Mere child's play. No, Stull was the stomping ground of the devil himself.

Satan appeared at Stull twice a year, on Halloween and the spring equinox, the legend maintained. The nexus of the activity was the crumbling shell of an old limestone church, abandoned since 1922, and the adjacent Emmanuel Hill cemetery.

In the cemetery, it was said, was buried a horribly deformed baby, stillborn in the mid-1850s. The baby's mother, a local woman, was a witch—who had been impregnated by the devil. It's not hard to imagine such a tale being stirred up in the middle of the nineteenth century, when folklore continued to prevail over science in many rural areas, upon the birth of a disfigured child. A grave marker in the cemetery bearing the name "Wittich"—awfully close to "witch"—may have contributed to the lore.

So, according to legend, on Halloween and other important pagan holidays, the devil would show up at the old limestone church next to the cemetery. He would climb a stone stairway and then appear before the cemetery to pay respects to his dead child.

Or how about this one? Soon after the town was established in the 1850s, a stable hand stabbed and killed the town mayor in a stone barn that eventually would be converted into the church;

the evil deed left a curse on the building, causing fires and turning crucifixes upside down. (The funny thing is that the town never had an official mayor.)

A few more: A large tree in the cemetery was used in ceremonies by devil-worshipping witches. The ghost of the demon baby ran about the cemetery, appearing as a werewolf-like creature. A good Christian boy from a nearby town embraced satanic rituals after visiting the place.

When these stories flared up in the 1970s, students from KU promptly made the pilgrimage west out of Lawrence to investigate the creepy reports. Young people poking around the cemetery reported being grabbed on the arm by unseen forces and experiencing unexplained memory loss. Two young men said a bone-chilling wind sent them running for their car, only to find the vehicle had moved to the opposite side of the highway and was facing the wrong direction. Another man claimed he was pushed to the ground by a fierce wind inside the limestone church.

Gossip reached a fever pitch, and soon Stull was a main attraction in Kansas. On March 20, 1978, the spring equinox, more than 150 people stood in the Emmanuel Hill cemetery, clutching one another and waiting for a glimpse of the devil. Similar groups gathered, most often on Halloween, in coming years; in 1988, five hundred people showed up on the spooky holiday. The massive scare-fest, which involved drunken college students and unruly revelers, resulted in overturned gravestones and damage to the historic church building.

Locals were not impressed. The vandalized tombstones marked the graves of their family members and ancestors. They contacted county law officials, who were ready and waiting on the next Halloween. The Douglas County Sheriff's Office stationed deputies around the cemetery, sending gawkers packing and writing tickets for criminal trespass. No-trespassing signs were hung, security fences were installed, and the grounds were patrolled nightly for some time. But Satan-seeking antics would continue, with a handful of cemetery intruders thrown in jail every Halloween and the *University Daily Kansan* providing a near-annual roundup on the latest developments at Stull. Another cemetery nearby also attracted attention, as the idea circled that the famous cemetery was meant to detract from the real gateway to hell, a few miles away.

In 1993, glam-rock band Urge Overkill sealed Stull's place in popular culture with the release of their EP *Stull.*

The title track, "Stull (Part 1)," describes a journey to the cemetery, the lyrics complete with three references to the number "six" ("666" being the "number of the beast" in the Bible) and a smattering of Charles Manson references for good measure.

Stull might have been a very rock-and-roll place, but—similar to the pope's avoidance of the place—The Cure refused to play a show in northeast Kansas due to Stull's reputation. At least that's how the story goes.

In 1996, when the roof blew off the church, attention shifted from the cemetery and its demon-baby to the limestone structure on the property. New legends emerged: Rain would fall around, but not into, the roofless church. Throwing a bottle at the church wall would tell you your fate; if it broke, you were headed to heaven, and if it didn't break—well, that was very bad news.

On Halloween night in 1999, reporters and TV cameras set up amid the spectators, much to the chagrin of cemetery owners, who knew that media attention meant more visitors, which meant more beer bottles to pick up.

By March 2002, cemetery owners had tired of the circus. Plus, they said, a church wall recently had fallen in, creating a serious hazard for mischievous youngsters wandering into an unstable structure. So, on Good Friday, they had the place demolished. It was a loss for historians who had rallied for a restoration of the nineteenth-century structure. It was a loss, too, of course, for KU students looking for cheap fun on October nights. But the cemetery remains, as do the ever-evolving legends surrounding the tiny town of Stull.

No word on whether the current pope would enter its airspace.

THE PATRIOT GUARD RIDERS

2005

As the casket containing the fallen soldier's body is lowered into the ground, demonstrators stand nearby, shouting vulgarities and carrying signs bearing hateful messages. But the disruptive group is neither heard nor seen by the soldier's grieving family members. Between the burial site and the protesters is a long line of bikers, clad in leather chaps, do-rags, and patch-adorned vests. The bikers—some bearded men, some ponytail-wearing women—keep their backs to the protesters, hold American flags and stare solemnly ahead, ignoring the ruckus behind them. Some of them rev the engines on their powerful motorcycles to drown the protesters' loud damnations. Their mission—to physically and audibly shield mourners from vitriolic demonstrations at military funerals—has been accomplished.

It's a scene that has played out hundreds of times throughout the nation since 2005. The biker group, which calls itself the Patriot Guard Riders, now numbers in the thousands and is represented in all fifty states; it formed in response to a Topeka church's controversial habit of showing up at soldiers' funerals across the country to denounce, among other things, gays in the military.

The Westboro Baptist Church, a Christian extremist group of about seventy-five in Topeka, attracted international attention by picketing soldiers' funerals to declare their belief that the entire country and its military were doomed for any acceptance of homosexuality. Eventually, state and federal laws would be passed placing restrictions on funeral-service protests; the establishment of a minimum distance between protests and services attempted to protect both freedom of speech and grieving funeral-goers. But, before that, a more grassroots approach was brewing with the aim of shielding mourners from upsetting protests.

In Lebanon, Missouri, members of the Combat Veterans Motorcycle Association were appalled that military families were being subjected to hate speech while burying their sons and daughters. Figuring that a large group of bikers, engines idling, could drown out a large group of demonstrators waving inflammatory signs, they began showing up wherever the Westboro church was expected.

Soon, Kansas bikers caught wind of the group's creative tactics. They joined in the cause, mulling over its possibilities in a small-town Kansas post of the American Legion, a national war veterans organization. In Mulvane, Kansas, in the summer of 2005, members of the American Legion Riders—the biker contingency of the veterans group—formed a committee and gave the operation a name: the Patriot Guard.

Its mission: to attend the funeral services of fallen American soldiers at the invitation of family members. And its two objectives in doing so: to show respect for fallen soldiers, their families and their communities, and to shield those in attendance from interruptions by protesters.

Soon, the Patriot Guard had its first mission. Westboro members had marked a military funeral in Chelsea, Oklahoma, on their calendar, so the Patriot Guard did the same. They contacted the family of the deceased and local law officials. Both were wary. The overarching sentiment was, "You are who, and you want to do what?" A group of bikers from another state descending upon a stranger's funeral seemed, well, odd. But, when made aware of the Westboro protesters' intended arrival, the soldier's parents ultimately extended an invitation to the Patriot Guard. Town authorities were much slower to warm to the idea. Suspicious of the group's motives, they stalled the Patriot Guard's entrance to the town, called in back-up police, and even positioned a sniper near the services.

But the Patriot Guard's first mission was a success, touching mourners with its quiet tribute and impressing local law enforcement with its tactical approach. It was a routine the group would perfect in coming months, as the operation went national as the "Patriot Guard Riders." Rules and procedures for legal, nonviolent "missions"—motorcycle rides to military funerals—were established, with all the attention to detail one might expect from a group of former soldiers. The process went like this:

Monitor "killed in action" press releases from the U.S. Department of Defense. Contact the fallen soldier's family and law enforcement. Scout the church and cemetery for a secure procession route and "staging area." Post an itinerary to the group Web site. Then, the day of the mission, suit up. The attire? Whatever the family requests. Maybe a special color of shirt, or something honoring an ethnic tradition. And don't forget to cover foul-language vest patches with masking tape—it's all about respect. Arrive an hour and a half before funeral services begin—even if that means leaving home at 4:00 a.m. on a frigid winter morning. At the service, salute the dead soldier. If protesters are present, turn your back to them, and hold the American flag high. Do not respond to a taunt or even a push. Sing, rev your engine, say the Pledge of Allegiance, but ignore the protester. Then, quietly pack up and ride home.

Just months after its inception, the Patriot Guard Riders were a familiar and welcome sight for members of the military community in small prairie towns, big coastal cities, and everything in between. In March 2006, as many as eight hundred bikers showed up on four hundred motorcycles to protect the funeral services of a Dodge City, Kansas, soldier. State captains from every corner of the country worked with the national board of directors to coordinate efforts (they even developed a uniform of sorts for missions—black hats for national officers and regional captains, red hats for state captains, maroon for ride captains, and blue for regular members). And the Kansas chapter took the common practice of waving American flags to the next level, assembling an arsenal of three hundred ten-foot flag poles and three-by-five-foot American flags—an impressive physical barrier between mourners and demonstrators. In 2006, the Kansas riders earned a place among the *Topeka Capital-Journal*'s "Kansans of the Year."

The group was so successful that its presence apparently deterred protesters who filed for permits to assemble and then never showed up with their incendiary placards. And, in many cases, the Patriot Guard Riders received requests to attend services with no known risk of protesters being present; bikers, many of whom were veterans themselves, would show up in the hundreds simply to show their support. The national organization's role even expanded beyond funerals to include "welcome home" events—say, providing a returning soldier with a roaring, flag-flying highway escort from the airport to his hometown. And, with certification as a nonprofit organization, the group accepted contributions to be funneled into travel costs and even the Fallen Warrior Scholarship Fund for children of military members who died in the line of duty.

During its first few years, the Patriot Guard Riders received hundreds of grateful letters from grieving families and community members. In the fall of 2006, a twenty-one-year-old Army soldier from Leavenworth was killed by a roadside bomb in Baghdad, Iraq, and hundreds of his hometown residents were expected at a visitation of the soldier's body at Leavenworth High. Word circulated that the Westboro church would be there, as well, and the Patriot Guard sprang into action. An area woman wrote the bikers to describe her experience that day.

"I had been at a meeting and was coming home around five that evening," the Leavenworth resident wrote. "When I got about three blocks away from the high school, traffic came to a virtual standstill. As I got closer to the school, my heart started to beat faster, and tears welled up in my eyes at what I saw. On both sides of the street in front of the school and up the side street were many people, each holding an American flag. Just quietly standing there, respectfully. It was one of the most beautiful sites I've ever seen. As I progressed I saw the horrible group from Topeka across the street from the school with their vicious signs. It brought a smile to my face to see the guard standing there with their backs to this awful group. I saw a group of bikes parked there with engines running and couldn't figure out what the deal was. What happened next made me laugh out loud. The terrible group started with their stupid chanting and suddenly all of the bike engines were revved drowning them out quite nicely! It was just a wonderful sight to see and hear."

The Leavenworth woman, a middle-aged Kansas native, applauded not only the Patriot Guard's dealing with the protesters, but its potential to combat misperceptions about her home state.

"One of the few times that I am ashamed to live here is whenever this terrible group is mentioned," she wrote. "I can say with 100% certainty to anyone reading this, this group's misguided opinions do not represent the people of Kansas. Thank you to the Patriot Guard for all you are doing."

THE FLYING SPAGHETTI MONSTER

2005

The world was created by a flying clump of spaghetti, and science students have a right to know.

That's the gist of a letter received by the Kansas State Board of Education in 2005. At the time, the board was embroiled in a contentious debate over science education standards in public schools. Conservative board members wanted to remove the phrase "natural explanations" from the state's definition of science; such a change would pave the way for the teaching of "intelligent design"—the idea that the natural world was created by some higher power—alongside the theory of evolution. The move toward such a change outraged many scientists, educators, and parents in Kansas and around the world, but the board's conservative majority suggested that curriculum changes were on the horizon.

Bobby Henderson, who was twenty-five and recently had completed a physics degree at Oregon State University, was among those who took issue with the Kansas board of education. He wrote them a letter explaining that, if intelligent design were allowed to be taught in schools, so too must the equally valid teachings of the Church of the Flying Spaghetti Monster.

"Let us remember that there are multiple theories of Intelligent Design," Henderson wrote, alluding to the fact that the vast majority of intelligent-design proponents adhered to the Christian faith. "I and many others around the world are of the strong belief that the universe was created by a Flying Spaghetti Monster. It was He who created all that we see and all that we feel. We feel strongly that the overwhelming scientific evidence pointing towards evolutionary processes is nothing but a coincidence, put in place by Him." (Henderson also asserted that humans evolved from pirates.)

This "scientific evidence," Henderson wrote, included lengthy written accounts of the world's creation, as well as a chart demonstrating correlation between occurrence of natural disasters and the decreasing pirate population since the nineteenth century. (He eschewed the laws of science by maintaining that this chart, "Global Average Temperature vs. Number of Pirates," indicated that the decrease in pirates had caused concurrent global warming.) Henderson also pointed out that observable evidence existed at the discretion of the Flying Spaghetti Monster, who might use "His Noodly Appendage" to alter scientific data.

In his satirical letter, Henderson threatened legal action were Flying Spaghetti Monsterism not given attention in science classrooms. Furthermore, he insisted that teachers wear "full pirate regalia" while teaching the theory, warning that the Spaghetti Monster otherwise would become very angry.

"If the Intelligent Design theory is not based on faith, but instead another scientific theory, as is claimed," he wrote, "then you must also allow our theory to be taught, as it is also based on science, not on faith. . . . I think we can all look forward to the time when these three theories are given equal time in our science classrooms across the country, and eventually the world; One third time for Intelligent Design, one third time for Flying Spaghetti Monsterism, and one third time for logical conjecture based on overwhelming observable evidence."

For good measure, Henderson included an ink drawing of his supposed god on a piece of notebook paper. A mass of noodles wound about two meatballs and sporting a pair of eyes, the spoof deity floated in the sky, surveying its creations.

Henderson sent the letter in May and received no response.

Eventually, he posted the diatribe to a Web site, and the Church of the Flying Spaghetti Monster—also known as Pastafarianism—gained nearly instant popularity. Bumper stickers, screensavers, and homemade movies devoted to the religion popped up in Kansas and across the country. Letters on behalf of the Church of the Flying Spaghetti Monster flooded the Kansas State Board of Education.

Members of the board finally wrote back to Henderson's letter, their comments ranging from tongue-in-cheek ("I was wondering if we could reverse the effects of global warming if we started breeding pirates") to outraged ("It is a serious offense to mock God"). One member of the board's political minority wrote to thank Henderson for the "wonderful comic relief" and to relay an update on the group's proceedings: Revised science standards had been drafted by the six conservative members, changing the definition of science from "seeking natural explanations" to "seeking logical explanations."

"That is why I think FSMism is able to be included," the board member wrote. "It is as 'logical' as any other theory." Meanwhile, the science teachers and professors who penned the original standards asked that their names be removed from the revised document.

Other academics from respected institutions in Kansas and around the world wrote to endorse Henderson's proposal.

"If Kansas schools (or any other public schools) are going to teach Intelligent Design as science, then they should clearly include the teachings of the First United Church of the Flying Spaghetti Monster," wrote a Kansas State University professor. "And, though there will be Pastafarians who disagree with me, I think that these schools should also include the theories of the Reformed Church of Alfredo and of the Cult of Oregano. That said, some ideas are too silly for even the Kansas public schools. For this reason, I would argue that we keep the Church of the Invisible Pink Unicorn out of the science curriculum. I mean, come on, now—that's ridiculous!"

A former research scientist wrote to Henderson about the Flying Spaghetti Monster's implications for the scientific method of carbon dating, used to approximate the age of objects in the natural world.

"It now seems obvious to me that the FSM must control the apparent half lives of all other radio isotopes, and similarly manipulates experimental results to produce the ages He wishes us to see," the scientist wrote. "What gives me tremendous respect for the FSM is that He clearly does this with a master plan in mind, such that 'dates' from entirely different isotope systems are all in miraculous agreement with one another. Especially amazing is that samples from geographically different locations, deemed to be from the same geological age on the basis of common fossils produce the same dates. This clever manipulation gives the impression of the evolution of progressively more advanced life forms through time, when the obvious truth is that the smarter creatures ran higher up in the mountains to escape the great (spaghetti sauce?) flood."

And physicist Stephen Unwin, author of *The Probability of God,* wrote to draw a line between the intelligent design movement and "what it means to be a Christian." "Yet, if supernaturalism be called for," Unwin wrote, "then the pasta family of theologies seems the most plausible, and unquestionably the tastiest with cheese."

In November 2005, the Kansas State Board of Education voted 6–4 to approve the changes to the science standards, a decision celebrated by some conservatives but largely lambasted around the world. With greater media coverage of the controversy came greater awareness of the Church of the Flying Spaghetti Number, and thousands of people jumped onto the Pastafarian ship. Homemade movies of the Flying Spaghetti Monster appeared online, and an "FSM" version of the ubiquitous Christian Ichthys fish adorned car bumpers. A computer game challenged the player to spread Pastafarianism by stretching "your noodly appendage toward the scurrying people" before time ran out. "Be sure not to make contact with the darkly-clad school administrators," the game warned. Henderson's Web site would receive millions of visits.

While the church was fun and games to most, Henderson made a mission of spreading the word. He wrote *The Gospel of the Flying Spaghetti Monster* in 2006 and raised considerable donated funds for the purchase of a "pirate ship" that might share Pastafarianism with the world. He responded to critics with the claim that his religion was the most peaceful in the world, having no fundamentalist factions and having caused no deaths, to his knowledge.

"Whether or not the Flying Spaghetti Monster actually exists is beside the point," Henderson wrote to visitors of his Web site. "It can't be proved either way, just as Christians can't prove the existence of their god. And there's no reason to try. We're all free to believe what we want."

In February 2007, new members of the Kansas State Board of Education voted to reverse the changes made to state science standards.

GREENSBURG

2007

Kansas is known for its twisters. Yeah, there's that movie about a girl named Dorothy, but Kansas tornadoes aren't just a Hollywood creation. The state rests in the middle of "Tornado Alley," where warm, moist air from the Gulf of Mexico clashes with cold, dry air from the north—setting the atmospheric stage for awe-inspiring thunderstorms that, sometimes, spawn menacing funnel clouds.

In early May 2007, numerous tornadoes came out to play throughout Tornado Alley. From May 4 to May 6, 123 twisters plagued seven states: Kansas, Colorado, Nebraska, Iowa, South Dakota, Oklahoma, and Texas. But, of the more than one hundred funnels, one dwarfed the rest: the Greensburg tornado.

On May 4, a dark, rotating monster of a cloud—two miles wide, with winds over two hundred miles per hour—roared into Greensburg, population one thousand, in central Kansas. The tornado, an unsurpassable EF5 on the tornado classification scale, leveled the town. Schools, churches, restaurants, banks, stores, homes: gone. By the time the storm passed, 95 percent of houses and businesses had been demolished, eleven people were dead, and many more were injured. The town's main attraction, the world's largest hand-dug well (aptly named "the Big Well") had seen its visitor center destroyed.

Greensburg, like many Kansas towns, was no stranger to tornadoes. In 1915, a tornado destroyed a Greensburg mine, and another large funnel cloud struck in 1923. On a June day in 1928, witnesses claimed, three twisters visited Greensburg at the same time. But never had the town seen such complete and utter destruction. The place seemingly had been wiped off the map.

The Greensburg tornado was by no means the deadliest for Kansans. A tornado killed thirty people in Andale in 1917 and, in 1955, another killed a record eighty-two people in the small town of Udall. Many lives were lost to later storms in Topeka, El Dorado, Hesston, and Andover. But rarely had a physical settlement been so thoroughly destroyed, nearly all of its hundreds of structures flattened, its trees broken in half, its vehicles crushed beneath debris, as Greensburg.

The place was declared a National Disaster Area, and volunteers in Kansas and beyond rallied to provide shelter, food, and clothing for the stricken residents of Greensburg who, suddenly, had nothing but the T-shirts on their backs.

Greensburg's future seemed as bleak as its flattened landscape. Like many small, agricultural communities in the Midwest, Greensburg had seen its population dwindling and its economy shrinking in recent decades. The tornado might have been the final blow, the end of the town. Why rebuild, when the town had been dying anyway?

A handful of leaders saw one good reason. They viewed the tragedy as an opportunity to put Greensburg back on the map in a major way. Greensburg was a blank slate, its buildings and very infrastructure wiped clean. And it was positioned in the heart of the Great Plains, the sun and wind unobstructed by mountains or tall buildings. Greensburg, the visionaries thought, could "go green" and become a leader in the trend toward sustainable building and city planning. With a bounty of solar and wind energy at its fingertips, and the necessity for much new construction, Greensburg had the rare chance to reinvent itself.

Townspeople had mixed feelings about such ambitions. Many of them wondered where they would get their next meal; environmentalism wasn't high on their priority lists. But the Greensburg city council soldiered on, adopting a resolution to build official city buildings to LEED (Leadership in Energy and Environmental Design) Platinum certification, the highest possible rating system by the U.S. Green Building Council. Once this beacon went out, declaring Greensburg's new direction to the rest of the world, support for a truly green Greensburg poured in.

First, there was the matter of infrastructure. The U.S. Department of Energy's National Renewable Energy Laboratory provided world-class counsel and resources for rebuilding the town's energy system, and an engineering firm developed an eco-friendly street-lighting system. A school administrator vowed to have the public school up and running by August—just three months after the storm, classes were in session in temporary buildings—and committed himself to a long-term, sustainable future for the school; he traveled to another state to view a model green school and helped create a state-of-the-art design for the school. The hospital manager continued work in temporary quarters, tending to her large, shaken staff and the heightened health needs of the community; she and her board embraced the idea of rebuilding a "green" hospital.

Then there was the matter of housing. A pioneer of sustainable insulation practices from Lawrence, Kansas, lent his expertise in the area of home energy efficiency; residents rebuilt their homes with geothermal heating and cooling systems and innovative concrete materials, achieving energy efficiency ratings that far outstripped what city code required. Some made use of trees felled by the tornado, turned into lumber when a sawmill company showed up with portable equipment to process the tree trunks. Eco-friendly homebuilders came from all over the country to meet the needs of residents attempting to balance green building and their checkbooks, in the process crossing numerous milestones for green residential building in the state of Kansas. A Florida builder traveled to and from Greensburg to guide construction of a silo-shaped, highly efficient structure; the building served as the first in a series of unique "Eco-Homes," model homes meant to serve as scientifically monitored "living laboratories" to teach both locals and "eco-tourists" about energy savings, building techniques, prices, and green products. Government agencies guided energy efficiency standards for a housing project of thirty homes—among the greenest "blitz-build" projects in the country.

Now, if the people of Greensburg stayed on, where would they work? The town's family-run tractor dealership—Greensburg's largest employer—rebuilt to the highest green standards, blazing a trail not just for local businesses but for similar dealerships throughout the country. A Missouri car dealer commuted hours each day to serve as a liaison to a giant automobile corporation, ultimately establishing a new business and a new, green building for the community.

Much of this progress was due to locals who dug their teeth into the rebirth of their town. A sixth-generation Greensburg resident chaired the fledgling Greensburg GreenTown, a nonprofit organization established to streamline and promote green initiatives within the town. And a new youth group, the Green Club, led initiatives for school recycling, turned Christmas trees to mulch, and campaigned for residents to use energy-saving compact fluorescent light bulbs; the club also constructed a sculptural bench from reclaimed metal and wood debris from the tornado.

But plenty of help came from outside volunteer efforts and large monetary donations. Architecture students at the University of Kansas designed a glistening modern building for the 5.4.7 Arts Center (named for the date of the tornado) at the center of town, while another class created sustainable home models and a home design book as resources for the town. Two recent college graduates moved to Greensburg and volunteered thousands of work hours to green projects. A major snack company donated a million dollars for the green construction of "the Incubator," a nexus of structures for ten local businesses, complete with solar panels and a rainwater collection system. A cleaning-product company gave $500,000 to the public school and its green goals. A telephone company donated $50,000 to the Eco-Homes project. A small U.S. toilet company donated four hundred dual-flush toilets to the community, a gift that would save the town more than two million gallons of water per year. A Wichita car dealer donated a compressed natural gas car, and partnering businesses donated a natural-gas filling station.

Throughout this long and complicated process, the city mayor and administrators spent countless hours learning about sustainable building and practices; they had bitten off the challenge of not just rebuilding a town from scratch, but of incorporating green practices at every opportunity. Governor Kathleen Sebelius was a frequent visitor throughout the first year after the disaster, championing the town's green ambitions and affording international visibility to its process. Kiowa County followed Greensburg's lead, applying green practices to county projects such as repairs to the county court-house—one of the few structures in Greensburg to survive the tornado. All the while, a national television network was there, filming a documentary of the town's journey of rebuilding.

Two years after the tornado, locals and U.S. Department of Energy representatives broke ground on the Greensburg Wind Farm (appropriate to the event, winds gusted at thirty-five miles per hour); they signed giant turbine blades in green marker as *Planet Green* stood by, filming its third season of the Greensburg documentary. The turbines would help power public buildings and businesses in the new town that had begun to take shape. As promised, all public buildings were LEED-certified at the platinum level, including the new school; it made use of daylight and natural ventilation, drawing 25 percent of its power from an on-site wind generator. Churches, small businesses, day care centers—the stuff of daily life—were visible again. Greensburg was coming back to life, in full color.

BIBLIOGRAPHY

Twelve Mile Creek

Hill, M. E. "Paleoindian Bison Remains from the 12 Mile Creek Site in Western Kansas." *Plains Anthropologist,* Vol. 41 (1996), No. 158, pp. 359–72.

Rogers, Richard A., and Larry D. Martin. "The 12 Mile Creek Site: A Reinvestigation." *American Antiquity,* Vol. 49, No. 4 (October 1984), pp. 757–64.

Thies, Randall M. "Earth, Wind, and Fire: Kansas Archeology." *Kansas Heritage,* Spring 1997, pp. 4–6.

City of Gold, Sea of Grass

Richey, W. E. "Early Spanish Exploration and Indian Implements." *Kansas Historical Collections,* Vol. VIII (1904), pp. 152–64.

Winship, George Parker (ed). *The Journey of Coronado.* New York: Barnes and Company, 1904.

Indian Removal

Clark, William. Letter to John Eaton, February 22, 1830. Kansas State Historical Society: William Clark Papers Collection #741, Records of the Superintendent of Indian Affairs Vol. 4, Item Number 210049.

Cummins, Richard W. Letter to General William Clark, April 2, 1831. Kansas State Historical Society: William Clark Papers Collection #741, Records of the Superintendent of Indian Affairs Vol. 6, Item Number 210046.

Miner, Craig. *Kansas: The History of the Sunflower State, 1854–2000.* Lawrence: The University Press of Kansas, 2002.

The Pottawatomie Massacre

"John Brown's Holy War," PBS, producer Robbie Kenner, 1999.

Townsley, James. "The Pottawatomie Killings." *Republican Citizen,* December 20, 1879, p. 5.

Quantrill's Raid

Riggs, Henry Earle. *Our Pioneer Ancestors—Being a record of available information as to the Riggs, Baldridge, Agnew, Earle, Kirkpatrick, Vreeland and allied families.* Ann Arbor, Mich., 1942.

Williams, Burton J. "Quantrill's Raid on Lawrence: A Question of Complicity." *Kansas Historical Quarterly,* Vol. 34, No. 2 (Summer 1968), pp. 143–49.

Exodusters

Hamilton, Kenneth Marvin. "The Origins and Early Promotion of Nicodemus: A Pre-Exodus, All-Black Town." *Kansas History,* Vol. 5, No. 4 (Winter 1982), pp. 220–42.

Miner, Craig. *West of Wichita: Settling the High Plains of Kansas, 1865–1890.* Lawrence: The University Press of Kansas, 1986.

Dodging Prohibition

Dykstra, Robert R. *The Cattle Towns.* Lincoln: The University of Nebraska Press, 1983.

The Hays Sentinel, March 23, 1877.

"Kansas Prohibition Law; Gov. St. John Claiming Credit Which He Does Not Deserve." *The New York Times,* February 19, 1882, p. 3.

Miner, Craig. *West of Wichita: Settling the High Plains of Kansas, 1865–1890.* Lawrence: The University Press of Kansas, 1986.

Reid, T. R. *The Washington Post,* July 2, 1987, p. A3.

The *Farmer's Wife*

Buhle, Mari Jo. *Women and American Socialism, 1870–1920.* Champaign: University of Illinois Press, 1983.

DeVault, Amy J. "The Farmer's Wife: Creating A Sense of Community Among Kansas Women." Association for Education in Journalism and Mass Communication Archives, September 2001, week 2, #50.

Endres, L. Kathleen, and Therese L. Lueck. *Women's Periodicals in the United States.* Santa Barbara, Cal.: Greenwood Press, 1995.

Miner, Craig. *Kansas: The History of the Sunflower State, 1854–2000.* Lawrence: The University Press of Kansas, 2002.

The Father of Basketball

Anderson, Dave. "Basketball's Papa Jimmy Remembered." *The New York Times,* December 19, 1991.

Miner, Craig. *Kansas: The History of the Sunflower State, 1854–2000.* Lawrence: The University Press of Kansas, 2002.

"Naismith, James (1861–1939)." *Encyclopedia of World Biography.* Farmington Hills, Mich.: Thomson Gale, 1998.

Wolff, Alexander. "Happy Hundredth, Hoops." *Sports Illustrated,* Vol. 75, No. 24 (December 2, 1991), p. 104.

Hatchet Job

Bader, Robert Smith. *Prohibition in Kansas.* Lawrence: The University Press of Kansas, 1986.

Grout, Pam. *Kansas Curiosities.* Guilford, Conn.: Globe Pequot Press, 2007.

Miner, Craig. *Kansas: The History of the Sunflower State, 1854–2000.* Lawrence: The University Press of Kansas, 2002.

Stratton, Joanna L. *Pioneer Women: Voices from the Kansas Frontier.* New York: Simon and Schuster, 1991.

First Flight

Haugen, Brenda. *Amelia Earhart: Legendary Aviator.* Mankato, Minn.: Compass Point Books, 2006.

Self-Guided Tour. Atchison, Kans.: Amelia Earhart Birthplace Museum, October 11, 2009.

Eisenhower's Roots

Ambrose, Stephen E. *Eisenhower: Soldier and President.* New York: Pocket Books, 2003.

Davis, Kenneth S. *Dwight D. Eisenhower: Soldier of Democracy.* New York: Smithmark, 1995.

The Goat-Gland Doctor

Fowler, Gene, and Bill Crawford. *Border Radio: Quacks, Yodelers, Pitchmen, Psychics, and Other Amazing Broadcasters of the American Airwaves.* Austin: University of Texas Press, 2002.

Lee, R. Alton. *The Bizarre Careers of John R. Brinkley.* Lexington: University Press of Kentucky, 2002.

Coal Miners' Daughters

Chinn, Jennie A. *The Kansas Journey.* Topeka: Kansas State Historical Society, 2005.

Grout, Pam. *Kansas Curiosities.* Guilford, Conn.: Globe Pequot Press, 2007.

"Kansas Law and Labor's Rights to Strike; Public Is Paramount, Governor Holds." *The New York Times,* May 29, 1920.

"Kansas Troops Out to Guard Workers." *The New York Times,* December 15, 1921.

"Topics of the Times." *The New York Times,* December 14, 1921.

The Dirty Thirties

"Farming in the 1930s: The Dust Bowl." Nebraska State Historical Society, www.livinghistoryfarm.org/farminginthe30s/water_02 .html (accessed October 14, 2009).

"Ford County Dust Bowl Oral History Project." Ford County Historical Society, www.skyways.org/orgs/fordco/dustbowl/ louissanchez.html (accessed October 14, 2009).

Miner, Craig. *Kansas: The History of the Sunflower State, 1854– 2000.* Lawrence: The University Press of Kansas, 2002.

Planes on the Plains

Chinn, Jennie A. *The Kansas Journey.* Topeka: Kansas State Historical Society, 2005.

Miner, Craig. *Kansas: The History of the Sunflower State, 1854– 2000.* Lawrence: The University Press of Kansas, 2002.

"Timeline: A Flight Through Time." Kansas Aviation Museum, www.kansasaviationmuseum.org/timeline.php (accessed October 8, 2009).

BIBLIOGRAPHY

Mental Revolution

"Karl Menninger, 96, Dies: Leader in U.S. Psychiarty." *The New York Times,* July 19, 1990.

Kneeland, Timothy, and Carol Warren. *Pushbutton Psychiatry: A History of Electroshock in America.* Santa Barbara, Cal.: Praeger, 2002.

Miner, Craig. *Kansas: The History of the Sunflower State, 1854–2000.* Lawrence: The University Press of Kansas, 2002.

Wishart, David J. *Encyclopedia of the Great Plains.* Lincoln: University of Nebraska Press, 2004.

Separate but Not Equal

Beyond Brown: Pursuing the Promise, DVD. PBS, 2004.

Smarsh, Sarah. "History Lessons." *MyMidwest,* January/February 2009.

Piece of the Pie

Grout, Pam. *Kansas Curiosities.* Guilford, Conn.: Globe Pequot Press, 2007.

Wishart, David J. *Encyclopedia of the Great Plains.* Lincoln: University of Nebraska Press, 2004.

Shotgun Artist

Appelo, Tim. "Kurt Cobain's Last No. 1 Hit." *Seattle Weekly,* December 25, 2002.

Burroughs, William S., and Allen Hibbard. *Conversations with William S. Burroughs.* Jackson: University of Mississippi Press, 2000.

Grout, Pam. *Kansas Curiosities.* Guilford, Conn.: Globe Pequot Press, 2007.

Popham, Peter. "Bill & Ralph's Excellent Adventure." *The Independent,* March 3, 1996.

City Divided

Abramowitz, Michael. "The War in Wichita." *The Washington Post,* August 9, 1991.

Maraniss, David. "Lessons of a Summer of Abortion Protests." *The Washington Post,* August 25, 1991.

"'Summer of Mercy' Costs in Wichita." *USA Today,* February 19, 1992.

Gateway to Hell

Gintowt, Richard. "Hell Hath No Fury." Lawrence.com, October 26, 2004.

Moran, Mark, and Mark Sceurman. *Weird U.S.: Your Travel Guide to America's Local Legends and Best Kept Secrets.* New York: Sterling Publishing, 2004.

The Patriot Guard Riders

Brooks, Steve. "On Guard." *American Legion Magazine,* November 3, 2008.

Feuer, Alan. "With a Chrome-Lined Cortege, the Patriot Guard Riders Pay Homage to Soldiers Killed in Iraq." *The New York Times,* May 29, 2006.

"Letters of Appreciation: Page Three." Patriot Guard Riders, www.patriotguard.org (accessed October 29, 2009).

Rojas, Ralph. Interview by author. Garden City, Kans., November 1, 2009.

BIBLIOGRAPHY

The Flying Spaghetti Monster

"Church of the Flying Spaghetti Monster." Bobby Henderson, www.venganza.org (accessed October 30, 2009).

Henderson, Bobby. *The Gospel of the Flying Spaghetti Monster.* New York: Villard, 2006.

Greensburg

Chiras, Daniel D. *Environmental Science.* Boston: Jones and Bartlett, 2006.

Queen, Bill, John Barrows, and Lisa Iannucci. *The Complete Idiot's Guide to Green Building and Remodeling.* New York: Alpha Books, 2009.

"Your Source for Everything Green in Greensburg, Kansas." Greensburg GreenTown. www.greensburggreentown.org (accessed October 31, 2009).

INDEX

ABOUT THE AUTHOR

Kansas native Sarah Smarsh is an assistant professor of English at Washburn University in Topeka, where she teaches creative nonfiction writing.